More

LEADERSHIP
LESSONS
OF
Jesus

More LEADERSHIP LESSONS OF Jesus

A Timeless Model for Today's Leaders

BOB BRINER & RAY PRITCHARD

BROADMAN & HOLMAN PUBLISHERS

Nashville, Tennessee

0–8054–1687–0

Published by Broadman & Holman Publishers, Nashville, Tennessee
Acquisitions & Development Editor: Leonard G. Goss
Page Design: TF Designs, Mt. Juliet, Tennessee

Dewey Decimal Classification: 253
Subject Heading: LEADERSHIP
Library of Congress Card Catalog Number: 98–24153

Unless otherwise noted, Scripture quotations are from the the Holy
Bible, New International Version, copyright © 1973, 1978, 1984 by
International Bible Society. Used by permission.

Library of Congress Cataloging-in-Publication Data
Briner, Bob.
    More leadership lessons of Jesus: a timeless model for today's lead-
ers/ by Bob Briner and Ray Pritchard.
        p. cm.
    ISBN 0–8054–1687–0 (hc.)
    1. Leadership—Religious aspects—Christianity. 2. Jesus Christ—
Leadership. 3. Bible. N.T. Gospels—Devotional literature.
    I. Pritchard, Ray, 1952– .II. Title.
    BV4597.53.L43B749 1998
    253—dc21

                                                    98–24153
                                                    CIP

                    1 2 3 4 5 02 01 00 99 98

This book is dedicated to Dr. Robert S. Folsom,
who has demonstrated the leadership lessons of Jesus
in sports, business, public service, and philanthropy.
I am grateful for his leadership in my life.
—Bob Briner

This book is dedicated to John and Helen Sergey,
missionaries for sixty years to the people of Russia.
—Ray Pritchard

TABLE OF CONTENTS

Acknowledgments   xi

Introduction   1

1   *How to Handle Opposition*   5

2   *Defining Your Mission Statement*   8

3   *Calling the Crowd*   11

4   *Guard Your Heart*   14

5   *The Power of a Rebuke*   17

6   *Jesus' Global Plan*   20

7   *The Strategy of Secrets*   22

8   *Setting Leadership Priorities*   25

9   *Timing Matters*   29

10 *Style, Substance, and Sympathy*   33

11 *Setting the Standard for Excellence*   36

12 *Moments of Compassion*   39

13 *Know Your Resources*   41

14	*The Joy of Order*	44
15	*Beginning with Gratitude*	47
16	*Handling Challenges to Your Leadership*	50
17	*A Floating Seminar*	53
18	*Beware of Rising Yeast*	55
19	*Managing the Big Picture*	58
20	*A Focus on Focus*	61
21	*Calculate Your Actions*	65
22	*On the Road Again*	68
23	*The Disciples' Final Exam*	70
24	*True Confession*	73
25	*How to Dispense News*	76
26	*Preparing for the Hard Times*	80
27	*Tough Love*	84
28	*Speaking to Inspire*	90
29	*Cultivating Loyalty*	93
30	*Bold Leadership*	96
31	*Why Intimacy Is Important*	99
32	*The Power of Outside Affirmations*	103
33	*Lingering on the Mountaintop*	106
34	*Control the Flow of Information*	109
35	*The Freedom to Fail*	112

TABLE OF CONTENTS

36	*Call Forth Faith*	114
37	*Only by Prayer*	117
38	*The Inner Circle*	121
39	*The Servant Leader*	125
40	*Children Are Welcome Here*	129
41	*The "Not Invented Here" Syndrome*	132
42	*How to Dispense Rewards*	136
43	*The Millstone Warning*	141
44	*Take Up Your Axe*	144
45	*Worth Your Salt*	147
46	*Marriage and Leadership*	151
47	*Overprotecting the Leader*	155
48	*The Truth About Flattery*	157
49	*Leading Versus Managing*	160
50	*Total Commitment*	164
51	*The Royal Order of Servants*	167
52	*Take Time for People*	170

ACKNOWLEDGMENTS

Once again, Dr. Ray Pritchard has proven to be an extraordinary writing partner. It is a joy to acknowledge, not only his major contribution to our joint writing effort, but also his contributions to my life as a friend, mentor, and spiritual guide.

Too, my wife Marty continues to be both inspiration and solid practical help in all I do. This certainly includes the writing of this book. I am grateful.

Jennifer Heldman has been a most faithful assistant, and I am appreciative.

Bob Briner

My friendship with Bob Briner is one of the great joys of my life. I am honored to partner with him once again. When people ask how I can pastor a church and write books at the same time, I tell them that I couldn't do it without the men and women who serve with me on staff. I am indebted to Kathy Duggins, Mia Gale, Sherrie Puknaitis, Phyllis Raad, and Cindy Todd for many kindnesses, large and small. They take care of many details and help keep my life organized. Special thanks to wife Marlene—my best friend and the person I trust more than anyone in the world. Nothing I do would be possible without her support. I pray for my three sons—Joshua, Mark, and Nicholas—that they might someday become men of God who lead as Jesus did.

Ray Pritchard

INTRODUCTION

He died well before His fortieth birthday. He never traveled more than 100 miles from His birthplace. His public ministry lasted less than four years. He left behind a handful of followers and told them to change the world.

They did. Twenty centuries have come and gone and the world is still changed because of what they did after He left.

When all the facts are fairly considered, we may safely say that Jesus Christ is the most effective leader the world has ever known. The tiny band He left behind has now become a worldwide fellowship numbering nearly two billion people in every nation on every continent.

How did He do it? We believe the Bible answers that question. This book is the second volume we have written on the leadership lessons of Jesus. The first volume covered the story of Jesus from the Gospel of Mark, chapters 1–6. This volume picks up the narrative at chapter 7 and carries it through chapter 10. As you turn the pages, you will follow Jesus as He moves slowly toward His date with destiny in

Jerusalem. Along the way you will discover how He took a group of very unlikely men and molded them into leaders who would carry on His work after He returned to heaven. You will have a front-row seat to some of the most amazing miracles ever recorded. After two thousand years no one can say how Jesus healed a blind man or fed four thousand people with only seven loaves of bread. We only know that He did it because He was and is the Son of God from heaven.

Keep reading and you will listen in as Jesus goes one-on-one with His harshest critics. These clashes with people in authority teach us much about how to respond to criticism without losing our sense of mission.

A few chapters later Jesus takes His disciples on a retreat to a place called Caesarea Philippi. There He challenges them to declare their personal commitment to Him and His mission. From that moment on He begins to speak openly to them about His coming death. This episode teaches us much about communicating our vision to our key associates and the importance of time and place in asking for a personal commitment.

In the last few chapters Jesus seems to be everywhere at once—healing a boy with an evil spirit, then settling a dispute among the disciples, then answering questions about divorce, and finally spending important one-on-one time with the man known as the rich young ruler. Our journey ends as Jesus travels the last few miles from Jericho to Jerusalem, healing a blind man along the way.

INTRODUCTION

We hope you will catch a glimpse of the most important Person ever to walk on planet earth. If you have dismissed Jesus as an irrelevant religious figure, think again. The Jesus you will meet in these pages is not some dim, distant icon. He is the Son of God and the greatest leader history has ever known. After twenty centuries His message still speaks to modern men and women.

We have intentionally kept each chapter short because we know how busy life is for most people. If you have a Bible handy, please take time to read the corresponding passages from Mark. By doing that you will gain much more from our comments and application.

Feel free to take your time reading this book. As authors, we won't mind if you underline sentences you like or make notes in the margin. Jot down questions that come to your mind. Take what we have written and apply it to your situation. Add your own comments. May this book inspire you to become a leader like Jesus.

Now we're ready to begin. Let's roll back the clock two thousand years and join Jesus and His disciples as unexpected visitors interrupt a pleasant meal. If you're ready, we now join a story in progress as Jesus teaches us how to deal with our critics.

CHAPTER 1

HOW TO HANDLE
OPPOSITION

The Pharisees and some of the teachers of the law who had come from

Jerusalem gathered around Jesus and saw some of his disciples eating

food with hands that were "unclean," that is, unwashed.

Mark 7:1

Leaders have a constant companion. It is opposition. If you lead, you *will* have those who oppose you. Be ready with answers for your critics, and do not let unjust or unwarranted criticism discourage you. (It is very important to be able to discern the difference between unjust or unwarranted criticism and constructive criticism given by caring friends, which is valuable to every leader.)

Opposition will often come in the form of attacks on your people, as was the case in the passage cited above. The Pharisees sought to distract and disrupt Jesus by attacking His disciples. Make no mistake about it—an attack on your followers is an attack on your leadership. As you defend your followers, you do two things. First, you defend yourself. Second, as your followers see you standing up for them, their loyalty to you and to your leadership is greatly enhanced.

While it is important to defend and speak up for your followers in public, this does not mean that you turn a blind eye to their actions that need reproof and correction. Followers *do* make mistakes. Some mistakes are honest. But some followers use their position to do bad things. Both need correction; the latter needs rebuke. In almost every circumstance, a leader will be wise to correct or rebuke followers in private or at least within an inner circle.

Note the way Jesus rebuked the disciples and the circumstances throughout the Gospels in which He did it. Jesus did not directly answer the criticism of the Pharisees, nor did He directly criticize their man-made rules. Instead, He dealt with the heart of the issue—man-made rules versus God's eternal law.

Nothing in this passage suggests that the Pharisees were wrong to establish certain traditions regarding ceremonial washings. Those traditions were meant to remind the Jews of their inner uncleanness and the absolute necessity of approaching God with a clean heart. But somehow that noble purpose had been twisted into an extrabiblical standard for judging others. When Jesus called them "hypocrites," it wasn't because of their rules, but because of their judgmental spirit that contradicted the very point of hand washing in the first place.

Jesus (1) responded to unjust criticism, (2) defended His disciples, and at the same time (3) refocused the issue away from His followers and back on His critics. Jesus did a masterful job of showing how a leader handles his critics without getting unnecessarily sidetracked.

CHAPTER 2

DEFINING YOUR MISSION STATEMENT

"You have let go of the commands of God and are holding

on to the traditions of men."

Mark 7:8

Effective leaders see beyond the traditional way of doing things and look for better ways. They do this, however, realizing that some things are sacrosanct, and they always keep the ultimate goal in mind. This is why it is so important to have a well-thought-out, closely defined, easily understood mission statement. Without this, even the most compelling and charismatic leaders get off track and go astray. A mission statement to which reference is constantly made is essential to quality leadership. Without this, personality, pride, and the exigencies of the moment will be diverting.

For Jesus, "the commands of God," doing His Father's will, constituted His mission statement. The "traditions of men" were never going to sidetrack Him from His goal. He was not to be diverted.

Again, the point to notice in verse 8 is *not* that the Pharisees were "holding on" to the traditions of men. We all do that to some extent because tradition helps us take the best of the past as a guide while we walk into the future. Jesus might be wrongly seen here as attacking all tradition. Instead, He excoriates the Pharisees for having "let go" of the commands of God. When you place your own traditions underneath God's will, they serve as a positive guide. But when the order is reversed, you end up exactly like the Pharisees—abandoning God's will for your personal agenda.

Note the specific example Jesus gives in verses 9–13. Evidently some Pharisees were using this man-made tradition of "Corban" to evade the clear teaching of Scripture to care for their parents. In light of the Fifth Commandment, this was a truly evil thing to do. First Timothy 5:8 reminds us that a believer who doesn't care for his own family is actually worse than an unbeliever. Christian leaders must never use their calling in business as an excuse to neglect their loved ones.

In a real sense, leaders of today have the same general mission statement. God's will should be the overall mission statement of every leader. Under this umbrella, our more personal mission needs to be spelled out specifically. An effective leader will understand his mission, be able to articulate it, and keep both himself and his followers from getting diverted. Vision, mission, and strategy are all necessary for quality leadership.

Be sure you have a mission statement for your life as well as for every leadership effort you undertake.

CHAPTER 3

CALLING THE CROWD

Again Jesus called the crowd to him and said,

"Listen to me, everyone, and understand this."

Mark 7:14

Words, at least as much as actions, are the tools of leadership and have awesome power. Great leaders throughout history have won significant victories by what they said and when they said it, and their words live long after most of their actions are forgotten.

Our key verse tells us that Jesus "called the crowd to him." There are times when leaders should not wait for an opportunity to speak; they should create one. When there are misunderstandings, when the opposition is getting its message out, when morale is low, or when morale is high are times when a leader will do well to call the crowd to himself.

Historians say that John F. Kennedy won the U.S. presidency by just such a calling of a crowd to himself. Kennedy, a Roman Catholic, spoke to a group of Protestant clergymen in Houston, Texas, and by his words defused most of their opposition to his candidacy. After this speech, his religion was never much of a factor in the election. His very narrow margin of victory points to the importance of one speech.

In that famous Houston speech Kennedy calmed the fears of the clergymen by professing his devotion to the Constitution of the United States and by appealing to the First Amendment guarantee of freedom of religion. His speech was effective because he (1) ventured into a potentially hostile audience, (2) faced the problem head-on, (3) appealed to common ground, and (4) in so doing, spoke through that audience to an entire nation.

About one hundred years earlier, another U.S. president delivered a speech that stirred the nation in Gettysburg, Pennsylvania. Abraham Lincoln, with only a few well-chosen words, actually reshaped American history and redefined the dream of democratic government. The Gettysburg Address is still widely quoted and beloved. Great speeches need not be long, but they must be thoughtfully prepared, timely, and spoken with forthright courage.

When a leader calls a crowd, the stakes go up. Be sure the time is right, and be sure you have something important to say. Don't become so mesmerized by your own oratorical powers that you overuse them. On the rare occasions when you do call people to you, your message must be both cogent and compelling.

Today, far too often, leaders neglect doing the hard work of learning to speak well. This is a big mistake. Even in our high-tech world, there will be times when a great, timely oral presentation will pay huge dividends. In some instances it can be the difference between success or failure. Be ready for occasions when your words will reveal the essence of your leadership.

CHAPTER 4

GUARD YOUR HEART

"Nothing outside a man can make him 'unclean' by going into him.

Rather, it is what comes out of a man that makes him 'unclean.'"

Mark 7:15

In light of verses 14–23, Jesus is challenging these religious leaders to consider the condition of their own hearts. It's easy to judge others as long as you don't look at yourself first. But judging will take on a different hue when you remember that you are not as good as you think you are. Jesus' whole point is: Don't sweat the food you eat—whether it is "clean" or "unclean"—because sin lurks inside you regardless of your diet or whether or not you washed your hands. *An effective leader guards his own heart because everything important in life comes from the inside out.*

Proverbs 4:23 states Jesus' point well: "Above all else, guard your heart, for it is the wellspring of life." The term *heart* in the Bible generally refers to the innermost part of life. It is the decision-making center, the source of motives, the seat of the passions, and the center of the conscience. It is truly the place "where life makes up its mind."

Proverbs has a great deal to say about the heart. It is the source of wisdom (2:10) and understanding (8:5), the origin of both deceit (6:14) and joy (15:30). The heart may backslide (14:14) or trust in God (3:5). It may be cheerful (15:13), prideful (16:5), bitter (14:10), haughty (18:12), or prudent (18:15). The heart may lust after an adulterous woman (6:25), it may rage against the Lord (19:3), and it may eventually be hardened against God altogether (28:14). The Lord tests the heart (17:3) because He knows what is in it (24:12), which is why the heart must be guarded all the time (4:23).

Jesus almost certainly had this verse in mind when He spoke to the Pharisees in Matthew 12:34b: "For out of the overflow of the heart the mouth speaks." This verse cuts both ways. Whatever is on the inside will eventually come out— whether good or bad. If a person's heart is dirty, he cannot produce purity in his life. Likewise, if the heart is stayed on the Lord, it will be seen on the outside eventually. The King James Version of Proverbs 23:7 reads, "As [a man] thinketh in his heart, so is he."

If you think angry thoughts, angry words are sure to follow.

If you fill your mind with sexual fantasies, your body will find a way to fulfill those desires.

If you dwell on your problems, they will soon overwhelm you.

If you feel like a victim, soon you will become one.

If you give way to worry, don't be surprised when you get ulcers.

If you focus on how others misunderstand you, you will soon become angry and bitter.

What goes in must come out. Sooner or later your thoughts translate into reality. You're not what you think you are; but what you think, you are. The flip side is also true.

If you focus on the truth, you will speak the truth.

If you look on noble things, nobility will mark your life.

If you seek out lovely things, your life will be lovely to others.

If you dwell on the right, the wrong will seem less attractive to you.

If you look for virtue, you will find it.

If you search for higher things, you will elevate your own life.

Recently a friend sent me this prayer from the *Book of Common Prayer*. It seems a fitting way to apply the words of Proverbs 4:23: "Almighty God, to you all hearts are open, all desires known, and from you no secrets are hid: Cleanse the thoughts of our hearts by the inspiration of your Holy Spirit, that we may perfectly love you and worthily magnify your Holy Name; through Christ our Lord. Amen."

CHAPTER 5

THE POWER OF A REBUKE

MARK 7:17–23

"Are you so dull?" he asked.

Mark 7:18

This passage is full of leadership lessons. The overriding one is that sometimes a sharp rebuke is a necessary and productive leadership tool. Jesus was no Milquetoast, namby-pamby leader. On several occasions He was exasperated with His disciples and let them know about it in no uncertain terms. In today's language He said, "Will you guys wake up? Aren't you ever going to get it? How many times do I have to explain it to you?" Those you lead will sometimes need to know you are not happy with them.

Note also the brevity of the question—"Are you so dull?" No doubt that stung. Just one quick question, then on to an explanation—perhaps with a bit of a sigh that He had to cover the same ground once more. *Wise leaders wait for the right moment, give a sharp rebuke, and then move on.* Foolish leaders keep repeating their criticisms endlessly, which leads not to better performance but to resentment and discouragement.

Good leaders use rebukes, especially the stinging ones, sparingly and strategically. They never use them to tear down or to ridicule for the sake of ridiculing. They always have a positive purpose. That purpose should never be to show how macho or clever the leader is or to give the leader ego gratification. Rebukes should hurt the leader as much as the one being rebuked.

One corporate leader always seemed to need a "punching bag," a person to be the target of his ridicule. Over a number of years, he "used up" many talented men and women, people he would bring into his inner circle and then subject to such constant and vitriolic ridicule that they would eventually move on, to be replaced by another object of his scorn. (The happy corollary to this is that several of these people went on to become very successful, even at a national level. But because of the incessant, unfair ridicule, their talents were lost to the original company.)

Note that the disciples' rebuke took place "away from the crowd." That is, Jesus didn't upbraid His disciples in front of the onlookers. In fact, He not only waited until they were in private, but He also waited until the question came from them. That way it would not seem as if He were out to get them or to humiliate them.

Timing is everything—both in giving compliments and criticisms. Jesus didn't hesitate to challenge His followers when He felt they weren't paying enough attention to what He was saying and doing. But He always did it in a way that preserved their dignity even while driving the painful point home.

Also note that the rebuke didn't involve what they didn't know, but rather what they should have known. It doesn't do any good to chastise your workers for failure to achieve goals that have never been explained to them.

Obviously, Jesus never made this kind of mistake. His rebukes were always for both the good of the person and the success of the enterprise. His example shows that a carefully considered rebuke, given with positive results in mind, is a leadership tool not to be neglected.

CHAPTER 6

JESUS' GLOBAL PLAN

Jesus left that place and went to the vicinity of Tyre.

Mark 7:24a

Tyre and Sidon were well-known centers of pagan culture in Jesus' day. They were commercial seaports on the eastern shore of the Mediterranean Sea that attracted traders from throughout the ancient world. The people of these cities were sophisticated, well educated, and deeply immersed in Greek culture, all of which was apparent in the many beautiful buildings, including elaborate temples dedicated to various heathen deities.

Is it perhaps significant that in the immediately preceding passage (7:14–23), Jesus speaks to the disciples about the importance of inner purity? His message on the sins that come from the inside would keep them from hastily judging the Gentiles. And inner purity is always important, but espe-

cially when going into areas of life where you know temptation will stare you right in the face.

The amazing thing is, Jesus went there. He wasn't afraid
to take His message to cities that others might consider "off-
limits" or too evil to reach. Some of His disciples no doubt
felt quite uneasy following Him to Tyre and Sidon. Most of
them had probably never been there before and didn't want
to ever be there again. However, going at this time prepared
them for His later Great Commission to take the gospel to the
ends of the earth.

Successful leaders have a plan that they pursue relentlessly.
A significant part of Jesus' plan was to demonstrate that the
gospel was not for the Jews only. Given the difficulty of travel,
the compactness of the area in which He moved, and the social
taboos against contacts with Gentiles, it is amazing how many
contacts Jesus had with non-Jews during His brief earthly lifetime: with the Magi, who attended His birth; the Gadarenes;
the Roman centurion; the Samaritan woman. Jesus met, inter-
acted with, and ministered very productively to a wide variety
of people. This is a powerful leadership lesson for today.

Given the constant "shrinking" of our planet and the
influx of immigrants into American society, the wise leader
will extend his or her leadership both to people beyond the
borders and to people within, who come from a different cultural and ethnic background. It is an absolute necessity to
plan with intentionality to interact productively with all the
people of God's wonderful creation.

CHAPTER 7

THE STRATEGY OF SECRETS

He entered a house and did not want anyone to know it;

yet he could not keep his presence secret.

Mark 7:24b

A very basic—perhaps *the* most basic—tool of leadership is information. How, when, where, and to whom information is dispensed is the very substance of leadership. The passage quoted above provides a starting point for an understanding of a leader's handling of information. In a human sense, *even Jesus* could not keep something a secret, even though He wanted to do so.

A place to begin understanding information, then, is the fact of the extreme difficulty of keeping anything truly secret. For a leader to think that he or she can do anything with anonymity is folly. For a leader to think he or she can hide any dynamic information for very long is foolishness. As Benjamin Franklin said, "Three can keep a secret if two of them are dead."

Do not try to build a leadership based on secrecy. It may work for a time, but inevitably it breaks down. In years of corporate life, I observed some leaders who thought they could best lead by sharing confidences among subordinates who were then supposed to keep them private. In the end, this never worked, and what generally happened was that staff would begin comparing "confidences" and find that they were each told the same thing on what they thought was an exclusive basis. Even worse, they sometimes learned they were told things that were mutually exclusive and contradictory. Confidence in this kind of leadership quickly erodes. An open honest style of leadership is always best.

It is practically impossible to hold any sort of newsworthy announcement, good or bad, for very long. In today's world it will "leak." It is always much better for a leader to decide how to break the news in the most productive way at the *earliest possible moment*. Otherwise, you will almost always find yourself responding to it rather than controlling it.

The most successful "holding" operation in which I was personally involved still ended in a painful situation. When the great tennis star Arthur Ashe discovered he had contracted AIDS from a blood transfusion, a very small number of his closest friends covenanted with him to keep his affliction a secret until he would go public at a time of his choosing.

There were some things he wanted to accomplish before he faced the huge public clamor he knew would ensue.

This worked for several months, but inevitably, he was confronted with disclosure before he was ready. A team of us orchestrated the resulting tumultuous press conference as best we could, but it was still very painful for Arthur and his family.

A secret is very hard to keep. News is almost impossible to hold. A wise leader will remember this. Even Jesus could not keep things secret.

CHAPTER 8

SETTING LEADERSHIP PRIORITIES

"First let the children eat all they want," he told her, "for it is not right

to take the children's bread and toss it to their dogs."

Mark 7:27

To understand this passage, it is necessary to know that the "children" to whom Jesus refers are His disciples. As a leader with a plan, He knew He had to use every teachable moment to instruct His followers about the plan. He would be with them for only a limited time. He had to give them as much as possible if they were to be able to function without Him. The plan, its execution, and its longevity had to take priority.

A true leader understands that he or she will not always be with his or her followers. Such a leader's goal is to enable followers to function as well as possible in the absence of the leader, whether the absence is temporary or permanent. Good leaders discuss this openly and unself-consciously, as Jesus did. Shortsighted leaders build and execute a program based on the fallacy that they will always be there. Their program only works in an optimum way when they are present and the followers serve through the leader.

From the very beginning, Jesus set out to lead in such a way that His followers would be able to productively carry on without His physical presence. The plan worked brilliantly. The church is the evidence.

Just as it is important to know that the "children" in the passage are Jesus' disciples, it is also important to know that the "dogs" are everyone else. In using the term *dogs,* Jesus was not denigrating the woman. He was making a powerful statement about priorities. He was saying, in effect, that compared to His basic mission, everything else became of very little import. He knew the priorities. He was going to fulfill the plan.

By responding to the woman the way He does, Jesus is not only instructing His disciples about His primary mission; He is also testing her faith. What might seem an insult is actually a way of saying, "Do you know who I really am and why I came?" Get this: When she said, "Yes, Lord," that's the only time anyone directly calls Jesus "Lord" in the Gospel of Mark. Hmmm. And it comes—not from the disciples—but from a Gentile woman. Perhaps she sees things more clearly than some of His closest followers do.

Further, the whole incident serves as a preparation for the later Great Commission. He came as the Messiah of Israel, but also as the Savior of the world. There is a true sense in which Jesus and the woman understood something about His mission that His disciples had not yet figured out—that He had come ultimately for the people of the whole world.

The woman, in one of the most prescient statements in all of Scripture, makes the case that Jesus can help her without detracting from His plan. He can solve her problem, can perform an act of charity, without in any way weakening His essential cause. This is a powerful and important leadership lesson.

A few years ago *Newsweek* ran a remarkable article on business leadership. One aspect of the article listed ways to spot a leader in trouble—a leader who had stopped leading. It pointed out that one of the easiest ways to identify a leader in trouble is to note the number of outside boards and charitable activities in which he or she is involved. Excessive involvement in activities outside the principle endeavor indicates a leader who either can't face the difficulties within or has become bored or burned out. In either instance, the enterprise suffers.

This syndrome shows itself often in both the local church and in higher education. When a pastor accepts more and more outside speaking engagements and increasingly looks for areas of service away from the local church, his leadership is in trouble. Anyone in higher education could spend every day attending a worthwhile off-campus meeting. He or she could do some very good work on boards and commissions. But excessive involvement off campus indicates a serious leadership gap on campus.

Watch for this syndrome in your own leadership. Watch for it in leaders of enterprises important to you.

Jesus showed us that we should do acts of charity that do not keep us from performing our mission. As was the case with the woman whose daughter Jesus freed from demons, involvement in ancillary charitable activities can be beneficial to the primary goal. If in the context of giving the best possible effort in your leadership role, you have the opportunity to contribute to a charitable effort, you should do it. However, the *most charitable* thing a leader can do is to give priority to his or her area of primary leadership.

This story is rich with meaning for all of us. It is a lesson about priorities, a lesson about having a global vision, a lesson about faith, and a lesson about using seemingly "unplanned" events as important teaching tools.

CHAPTER 9

TIMING MATTERS

Then Jesus left the vicinity of Tyre and went through Sidon, down to the

Sea of Galilee and into the region of the Decapolis.

Mark 7:31

Jesus did not take the "normal" or expected route back from Tyre and Sidon. He seems to have gone east and then south through Decapolis, skirting the northern border of Galilee, His "home territory." Why? Two reasons.

First, His many miracles had caused a movement to arise to make Him king by force or acclamation—neither was part of His plan. Second, He also knew that there was rising opposition to His ministry among the Jewish leaders. Because He knew the time was not right to force a public confrontation, and because the crowds in Galilee didn't really understand who He was, He elected to temporarily bypass His "home territory" in favor of the Decapolis, cities which had previously been hostile to His message.

To understand the full leadership import of this Scripture, read Mark 5:17b–20: "Then the people began to plead with Jesus to leave their region. As Jesus was getting into the boat, the man who had been demon-possessed begged to go with him. Jesus did not let him, but said, 'Go home to your family and tell them how much the Lord has done for you, and how he has had mercy on you.' So the man went away and began to tell in the Decapolis how much Jesus had done for him. And all the people were amazed."

The last time Jesus had been in the Decapolis, the ten cities, the people had begged Him to leave. This time, evidently, they were happy to have Him there and begged Him to place His healing hand on their friend. What had changed? It seems obvious. Jesus had shown great wisdom and great leadership by forbidding the formerly demon-possessed man to accompany Him. Instead, by asking him to remain in his home region and to tell what Jesus had done for him, the man became a powerful and believable agent for the Lord. Jesus demonstrated that quality public relations based on truth and timely, well-directed publicity are valuable leadership techniques. He practiced both with great skill.

The two visits Jesus made to the Decapolis demonstrate some other basic leadership precepts. On His first visit the people asked Him to leave, and He did. He was wise enough to see that a proper foundation for His work had not yet been laid. Instead of trying to force Himself and His message on them, He left. But He left an important representative to prepare for His next visit.

When the time was right, He returned and ministered with great effect. What a lesson! A wise leader will not try to force his leadership on people who are not ready.

Strategic retreats are part of the smartest leadership. While a wise leader will not force his or her program, neither will a wise leader give up on a situation without allowing time and the laying of a better foundation to make the situation tenable. In our business of distributing sports television, we saw this principle work to good effect. In the 1970s Korea became a viable television market. We went there hoping to sell the Korean networks a major package of tennis events. However, the Koreans told us they had absolutely no interest in the sport of tennis and we should, in effect, get lost.

We left but continued to be in touch with them, showing them how well tennis worked on television in other Asian countries, particularly in Japan—a country they always try to emulate. Our patience and foundation-laying paid off in a big way, and Korea has become one of the best international markets for televised tennis, as well as other sports.

Important leadership lessons then are: (1) don't try to force your leadership or your program where there is not readiness for it; (2) use quality public relations and education to lay a good foundation; and (3) at the proper time, try again.

Remember both of Jesus' visits to the Decapolis and the leadership lessons they teach. Jesus never did anything haphazardly; even His "small" decisions always had a larger purpose behind them.

CHAPTER 10
STYLE, SUBSTANCE, AND SYMPATHY
MARK 7:33–35

After he took him aside, away from the crowd,

Jesus put his fingers into the man's ears.

Mark 7:33

In the passage cited above, the key phrase is "away from the crowd." As we survey the miracles of Jesus, we see that His miracles had two primary purposes. One was to perform an act of love and mercy for the recipient. The other was to advance the plan by teaching lessons important to the plan.

A leader needs both style and substance, but it is important to never put style over substance. The real, tangible results are what count the most. Jesus performed miracles as a completed work. Substance. He also paid great attention to the "style" in which the miracles were performed. But even in paying attention to style, He always resisted the "grandstand play." He never did anything for self-aggrandizement, but always to glorify the Father and to do the will of the One who sent Him. Both substance and style should advance the cause.

Today's leaders need to carefully consider the time and setting for announcements, product introductions, and demonstrations. Is the overall plan advanced better by pointing narrowly to close associates or by aiming broadly to influence a wider audience? The accomplishment of the primary goal should be the leader's focus.

Consider another important lesson Jesus teaches leaders in this passage. By touching the man's ears, Jesus shows His sympathy with the man. In the previous miracle, Jesus casts the demons out of the woman's daughter when she isn't even present. Here Jesus touches the ears, then touches the man's tongue with His own spittle—both very intimate, extremely personal gestures. Why? The first miracle shows His power to heal over a great distance, the second His intimate involvement with this man's suffering. Wise leaders recognize that not all decisions should be made in the same way, not all problems handled in an identical fashion.

Also, note that He sighed. An amazing statement—the only time such a thing happens and is recorded. He sighed—not out of the difficulty of the case, but in deep compassion with this man's suffering—and perhaps by extension for the suffering of the whole world. Remember, Mark never records an irrelevant detail. Here is proof that Jesus was "touched with the feeling of our infirmities."

Sometimes leaders must do things quickly and then move on. At other times they will stop, take their time, and by their actions and their words, demonstrate deep personal concern. There are no "rules" for when to do what—only the recognition that leadership demands different responses on different occasions.

When the president speaks from the Oval Office, he always wears a business suit and speaks with dignity. But when he visits the state fair he takes off his coat, sits down, and eats corn on the cob with the ordinary folks. Which picture makes the front page the next day? Unless he's declaring war, it's always the president with the people. In this passage full of good lessons for leaders, Jesus shows us more of His "human" side even while performing a mighty miracle.

CHAPTER 11
SETTING THE STANDARD FOR EXCELLENCE
MARK 7:36–37

People were overwhelmed with amazement.

"He has done everything well," they said.

Mark 7:37

Jesus was, of course, the most amazing person who ever lived. He did everything better than anyone else ever has or ever will. He continues to do this as He "prepares a place for us," daily intercedes on our behalf, and holds the world in place by the power of His Word.

We can never hope to overwhelm and amaze others the way He did, with His greatness and power. For leaders of today, however, the good news is that it takes relatively little to overwhelm and amaze. Our society has grown so far away from the standards Jesus set that today's leaders can stand out in stark and positive contrast to those around them by doing even the small things well. And doing the small things well is the basis for doing the big things well—the basis for quality, effective leadership.

Leaders used to lead by both precept *and* example, beginning with the small things. There are CEOs whose companies have high-sounding and noble mission statements, but whose own conduct and deportment in the small things is less than amazing or overwhelming. Unfortunately, the same kind of thing is often observable in churches. Some have a wonderful, expressive mission statement declaring that the intention of the church is to produce "caring servants"; but their staff, at the highest level of church leadership, fails to reflect that in the way they perform in the small, everyday interactions with people.

When a leader is always late, doesn't answer mail or return phone calls, or fails to say thanks, this is eventually reflected in the effectiveness of his or her leadership. Sooner or later, the enterprise suffers. These are small things, but they turn into big things. Fortunately, these are things all of us *can* do well. It only takes commitment and resolve. And if we, as leaders, will do these small things well, not only will our enterprise benefit, people will be overwhelmed with amazement because so few people bother these days.

Reflect on the truth of the parables of Jesus which teach that faithfulness in small things and trustworthiness in the seemingly mundane things of life lead to greater opportunities. Therefore, leaders who take care of the small things well in a small arena will most often have the opportunity to lead in a larger arena. Little things do mean a lot.

In Jesus' case, His overwhelming approval from the masses came because of His wisdom, His compassion, His sense of divine calling, and the unquestioned purity of His motives. It wasn't just His miracles, because even false prophets could work miracles (see Matt. 7:21–23). Miracles alone don't produce this kind of response.

We look at Jesus and think, "I could never perform the miracles He did." That's true, but any of us could—with the power He provides—live a life of giving and, in a small way at least, have a Christlike impact.

CHAPTER 12

MOMENTS OF COMPASSION

"I have compassion for these people; they have already been with me

three days and have nothing to eat."

Mark 8:2

Compassion is an absolute necessity for quality leadership. Without it, leadership becomes cold, self-serving, and tyrannical. The kind of leader who produces lasting, positive results, particularly results that last for eternity, *will* have compassion. If you do not genuinely care about those you lead and those you serve, get out of leadership. You will do more harm than good.

Here is a case where a leader acted wisely and with compassion simply because something needed to be done right then. Sometimes leaders do have to curtail their immediate plans in order to take care of those who follow them. For example, you might have to postpone a meeting, reschedule a trip, or come home early from vacation because of unforeseen problems among your workers. In such cases, the leader can either light a candle or "curse the darkness." Jesus used this opportunity to (1) meet the people's needs, (2) re-teach His disciples about His power to provide for His people, and (3) work an amazing miracle they would never forget. In so doing, He turned what could have been a disaster into a startling triumph.

There is a secondary lesson here as well. This is the second feeding miracle in Mark. The first one—recorded in Mark 6:30–44—happened in Israel and involved a mostly Jewish audience. This one happens in Decapolis and involves mostly Gentiles. Some critics have imagined that the Gospel writers for some reason invented two stories, but a cursory comparison shows many points of contrast.

Leaders shouldn't be surprised when the same problems crop up again and again. If you deal with big crowds of people in the desert, don't be surprised when they get hungry and thirsty.

Sometimes leaders complain or act surprised when problems recur, sometimes with different audiences. It's not always a sign of bad planning that problems repeat themselves.

Jesus doesn't appear bothered or flustered in this passage any more than in the earlier one. He simply sees the need and moves to meet the need. What a simple lesson, but how much we need it!

CHAPTER 13

KNOW YOUR RESOURCES

"How many loaves do you have?" Jesus asked. "Seven," they replied.

Mark 8:5

An effective leader knows the extent of his resources. He is willing to ask the necessary questions in order to know. He doesn't rely on guesswork. He gets the numbers from the ones who know.

Obviously, Jesus knew the answer to the question before He even asked. Just as obviously, He wanted to involve His disciples in the situation and make them a part of the undertaking to solve the problem. He could, of course, have handled everything with just a divine word. By not doing it this way, He provided leadership lessons for His disciples and for us as well.

Historians tell us that General Robert E. Lee constantly asked his subordinates—even on the very day of his surrender at Appomattox—"What opportunities do we have before us?" He did this (1) in order that he might not miss any strategic possibilities, and (2) to train his officers to see the larger picture. When Jesus asked the disciples how many loaves they had, He immediately involved them in the solution to the problem at hand. Good leaders must know what they have, and they must train their followers to start with whatever they have on hand.

A wise leader looks for ways to involve those he leads in as many productive activities as possible. A leader's job is not to do, but to get things done. A wise leader will resist the impulse to do things himself in favor of allowing his followers to learn and grow by doing it. A leader should, to the extent possible, do *only* those things which *only* he or she can do. The other things should be delegated.

When a leader becomes involved in doing nonleadership things, except for the purpose of teaching, the enterprise suffers. A leader's time should be devoted to planning and meeting the overall needs of the organization, delegating, inspiring, motivating, and teaching. Allow others to grow by allowing them to learn by doing.

In this story Jesus, the leader, sees the need and decides that He must meet it. He then expresses His commitment, which His followers think is futile. He surveys their resources, divides the crowd, performs the miracles, uses His disciples to serve the food, and later uses them to clean up afterwards. In short, Jesus here does what only He can do—

a miracle—and involves His disciples in every other part of the event. That's truly good leadership.

Note that Jesus was not offended or angered by their doubt. He knew that doubt could become a wonderful teaching tool. Seen in purely human terms, their paltry resources were nothing against the overwhelming need. But they had evidently forgotten the earlier miracle or doubted Jesus could do it again, perhaps thought that He wouldn't do it again in Gentile territory. In any case, leaders must be prepared for doubt and skepticism from within the inner circle. Such a moment provides a supreme test of the leader's vision . . . and his self-control. If he loses his cool, he loses their respect and also the chance to show them how a leader reacts wisely under pressure.

Jesus, who could do all things well, made sure His disciples got the experience in doing things themselves. This would serve them and their vital enterprise well after Jesus was physically removed from their midst. This is a valuable lesson for all leaders.

CHAPTER 14

THE JOY OF ORDER

He told the crowd to sit down on the ground.

Mark 8:6a

Note the leadership principles in Mark 8:6:

1. *He* told the crowd: Personal leadership
2. He *told* the crowd: Clear instruction
3. He told *the crowd*: Mass communication
4. To sit down on the ground: Order out of chaos

Think about what would have happened if Jesus hadn't imposed order. There would have been a wild stampede as the food was handed out. Some would have gotten more than they needed while others would have gone hungry. A beautiful miracle would have been lost in the dust of a Middle Eastern food riot.

We serve a God of order. In the very act of creation, God brought order out of chaos. Jesus' leadership is characterized by the creation of order. Ours should be as well.

A leader's first responsibility is to bring about order. Without order, leadership is mundane and ineffective. Without order, planning is wasted. Leadership and order are inextricably intertwined.

It is important to realize that some people are gifted with an innate sense of order, and some are not. Leaders and potential leaders need to do an objective self-analysis about this area of their lives. Wise leaders and those who work with them will make sure that an otherwise gifted leader who lacks organizational skills will have the assistance of someone who is responsible for "picking up the pieces," making sure that order and orderliness are maintained.

This is particularly important in churches. Gifted pastor-teacher spiritual leaders are often not given to administration and to the orderly conduct of the church activities. In this sort of situation, it is vital that the senior pastor recognizes this and that someone is brought in as an administrative pastor to create and maintain order. The wise senior pastor will not resist this kind of help, but will welcome it and revel in it. An orderly context will make his other leadership gifts that much more effective for the kingdom. This is true in other fields as well, such as business and education. Do whatever it takes to eliminate any shortfalls in this area.

Sometimes leaders resist this because they feel insecure or somehow inadequate and tend to treat others as competitors and not team members. Sadly, they end up operating at 30 percent efficiency because they won't dare let anyone else "manage their weaknesses."

A home, particularly a Christian home, should be orderly. The leaders of the home, the father and the mother, should make order a high priority. Christian social psychologists tell us that disorder in the home robs us of a sense of joy. Without order, there can be no meaningful plan for the household to progress toward godliness.

Now, it is important to understand that order does not mean mindless regimentation enforced with martinet-like strictness. It does mean a neat, clean, and orderly residence, a reasonable schedule, obedient children, and considerate and loving adults. This kind of home produces and encourages leadership outside the home, advancing God's kingdom on two fronts. Fathers and mothers make an orderly home a priority. Leadership begins here.

To some people, taking the time to bring order out of chaos seems to be a heavy burden. "Just go with the flow." "Let the Spirit lead." "Don't worry about the details," they say. Yet in the end, the price of taking time to do things "decently and in order" is always lower than the price of letting things take their own course.

Our Heavenly Father is a God of order. Jesus' leadership is characterized by commitment to order. We must commit to it as well.

CHAPTER 15

BEGINNING WITH GRATITUDE
MARK 8:1–10

When he had taken the seven loaves and given thanks, he broke them and

gave them to his disciples to set before the people, and they did so.

Mark 8:6b

The resources of any leader are finite. Often they will seem inadequate for the situation. Jesus, who, of course, had infinite resources, teaches us in this passage that we are to be thankful for what we have and to use what we have in faith. Leaders are not to become paralyzed by the difficulty of circumstances.

Using what we have, with thanksgiving, and moving positively ahead in faith is often the beginning of a great leadership triumph. This is in no way advocating rash and foolish action; and as we have said before, strategic retreat is often the most positive thing we can do. The call here *is* for a leadership that will act, that will chip away at the problem with the resources at hand. Tom Peters calls this "Ready, fire, aim."

Many great and enduring enterprises, most great and enduring churches have begun with "seven loaves" and "a few small fish," resources totally inadequate for the situation. A visionary leader focused on what was at hand rather than on what wasn't, and began to build. Great things ensued. What often happens when we begin to use what we have is that others will be inspired to join and help. New resources are found and are brought to bear. In feeding the four thousand, God supplied. He still supplies needs, but most often responds to faith in action. When we move, He moves. A leader moves and directs his followers to move in a positive way. Doing nothing accomplishes nothing.

Don't miss the other vital leadership lesson in this passage. Jesus didn't wring His hands over the small supply and the enormity of the task; He gave thanks for the loaves and the fish. Why? Certainly to acknowledge that even the little that they had came from the gracious hand of God. Ungrateful leaders will never accomplish great things because ingratitude saps the soul of its creative strength. You can either sit around moaning about what you don't have, or you can give thanks and get to work with what you do have.

Note that after the feeding there were seven large baskets—a different word from the one used in Mark 6—containing leftovers. That is, there was more at the end than there was at the beginning—even after feeding four thousand men.

Thus it always is when leaders move to meet genuine needs, trusting in God, with grateful hearts, beginning where they are with the resources on hand. This kind of miracle happens in various ways every day as godly men and women do what Jesus did in the wilderness of Decapolis.

God blessed Jesus' supply and effort. Today He blesses those who take what they have, put it to work, and trust Him to make up whatever they lack.

CHAPTER 16

HANDLING CHALLENGES TO YOUR LEADERSHIP
—————— MARK 8:11–13 ——————

The Pharisees came and began to question Jesus. To test him, they asked

for a sign from heaven.

Mark 8:11

Leaders will always be questioned and tested. I have known some leaders who feel that after they have demonstrated competence over time, they should be immune from challenging questions and testing. This is an unrealistic expectation. Unfortunately, people are never content with yesterday's brilliance, last week's good program, or last Sunday's wonderful sermon.

It is very instructive to note that the Pharisees began to question Jesus, test Him, and ask for a sign from heaven immediately after He had fed four thousand men with seven loaves and a few fish! By this time in His ministry,

Jesus had already done many other miraculous things in highly public settings. The word of these feats had spread far and wide. Still, the Pharisees questioned Him and wanted a sign from heaven.

Jesus knew that their motives weren't good and their request wasn't sincere. Their questioning was indeed a kind of trap meant to throw Jesus off course. Somehow they had managed to rationalize everything Jesus had already done. Either miracles were faked or staged, or perhaps they were just lucky coincidences. So now they asked for some showy demonstration. The implication was: If you do this, then we'll believe you. But in reality their minds were already made up.

Sometimes hearts can become so hardened that nothing we do or say can change them. Jesus recognized that, refused to argue, sighed deeply (one supposes, with a mixture of resignation and sadness), and moved on.

The best leaders can recognize the difference between legitimate questions and objections meant simply to throw you off track. One useful sign may be: If someone comes and asks you for "just one more" proof that your plan is going to work, think carefully before you offer that "one more" proof, lest you get caught in the trap of endlessly trying to please people who will never be pleased no matter what you do.

A dangerous and defeating response to this kind of questioning and testing is to say, "Okay, you want a sign? I'll give you a sign," and then to go out and do something that is not part of the plan and does not really further it, thinking it will silence the questioning critics. It never works. These kind of critics will not be silenced. It is much better to respond the way Jesus did—"sigh deeply" and move on.

As he often does, Billy Graham has much to teach us here. After a remarkable lifetime of humble dedicated service, after unprecedented success in preaching the gospel over many years, there are still those *within the church* who question him and test him. Dr. Graham almost never responds. He seems to "sigh deeply" and move on.

Dr. Graham relentlessly pursues his plan and his program. He is not distracted. He does not get in name-calling contests. He does not get defensive. He conducts another crusade. He preaches the gospel. What an example! It is a leadership lesson of Jesus, played out for us by a contemporary leader. We very much need to appropriate this lesson for our own leadership styles.

Never think you will escape questioning and testing. Based on your leadership record, the questioning and testing may be unfair and unwarranted. However, it will come. Be ready for it. Be ready to "sigh deeply" and move on with the plan God has called you to execute.

CHAPTER 17

A FLOATING SEMINAR

The disciples had forgotten to bring bread, except for one loaf they had

with them in the boat.

Mark 8:14

A wise leader certainly arranges times for formal teaching, set aside for the dispensing of vital knowledge and instruction. However, the most effective teaching often happens when an alert leader takes advantage of one of those exceptional teachable moments that occur spontaneously.

In the incident cited above, the disciples obviously had not done what they should have done. They should have had a sufficient supply of bread for the trip across the Sea of Galilee. Jesus could have used this failure to teach them a lesson about supplies, logistics, checklists, and organization. He could have lectured them about the importance of paying attention to details. He could have said, "Just because my

Father made possible the feeding of four thousand with seven loaves, don't think this relieves you of the responsibility to plan for our own needs."

This *is* a lesson that some followers of some leaders need to be taught. Some followers develop such confidence in particularly effective leaders that they become careless in their own duties, thinking that the brilliance of the leader will always bail them out. However, Jesus chose to teach a much more fundamental lesson. From His example, we should learn to use those precious teachable moments to accomplish the greatest good.

At this moment in His ministry, Jesus faced the reality of an ever-growing opposition from the religious leaders of Israel. Their malignant hostility posed a greater threat to His mission than any lesser problems regarding logistics or scheduling. Seizing the moment, Jesus ignored those important areas in order to instruct His disciples about something that was both *important* and *crucial* to their future success. In doing so, Jesus took a teachable moment and turned it into an unforgettable floating seminar.

CHAPTER 18

BEWARE OF RISING YEAST

"Be careful," Jesus warned them. "Watch out for the yeast of the

Pharisees and that of Herod."

Mark 8:15

To know and understand your enemy is an important admonition. Good leaders understand the factors that will mitigate against the success of their enterprise.

There is one school of leadership that says, "Forget the competition. All we need to do is to focus on what we are doing, and we will be okay. Don't get distracted by what others are doing." This sounds good and *is* good, but only up to a point. You certainly don't want to become so mesmerized by what your adversaries are doing and get so caught up in countering them that you fail to execute as well as you possibly can. However, Jesus teaches us, as He taught His disciples here, that knowing your enemy will help you to overcome.

The best professional teams work endlessly on perfecting their own execution. At the same time, there are scouting operations which seek to know as much as possible about how their opponents play the game. The execution is then honed to be the best possible counter to their opponent's style of play. You don't neglect preparing to do your best, but you also learn how to best do it relative to your competition.

Our company is a relatively small one with only about 150 employees. On occasion we have found ourselves competing against some of the giants of international business. By careful observation we learned that their "pitch" would almost always center on their vast staff resources, on how many people they could bring to bear on a particular situation. By knowing about and understanding their tactic, we learned at least one way to try and counter it.

When faced with competing against a very large company, our approach to an athlete would be: "We can't promise huge numbers of people for your project, but what we can promise is that our very top people will be very personally involved. If you go with us, you won't be dealing with 'lieutenants.' You will have seasoned 'generals' taking daily personal responsibility for the success of the project." In other words, my partner and I would promise our own hands-on involvement. This often worked and we sometimes won against the giants. If we had not known about our competition, we could not have crafted a viable strategy.

Note another important point about Jesus' teaching. He draws the lesson by moving from the familiar to the unfamiliar. Seeing the disciples' one loaf of bread, He uses yeast to illustrate the evil intentions of Herod and the Pharisees.

This was a powerful illustration for two reasons. Every one of the disciples would have known all about yeast because it was so commonly used. Also, everyone understands that it only takes a little yeast to leaven an entire loaf of bread. It was the perfect illustration for the point Jesus wanted to make—a common substance known to all whose properties illustrated the pernicious nature of the evil working against them.

In telling them to "Watch out!" Jesus is teaching them that (1) there really are enemies out there, (2) the enemies are crafty and hard to spot, and (3) constant vigilance would be required to defend against them.

Wise leaders find simple ways to alert their followers to the dangers they face. In this case the disciples didn't at first grasp what He was saying. That only reinforces the importance of leaders' constantly teaching, teaching, teaching, and not assuming that their words are always immediately understood.

CHAPTER 19

MANAGING THE BIG PICTURE

MARK 8:14–21

"Be careful," Jesus warned them. "Watch out for the yeast of the

Pharisees and that of Herod."

Mark 8:15

Leadership, almost by definition, relates to the big picture. Successful leaders cannot get bogged down in minutiae. In most instances the details *must* be delegated. There are, however, some seemingly small things that, left unattended, will become big things and will prevent maximum good from occurring. In the verse above, Jesus was teaching about these kinds of things, the nonnegotiables.

A wise leader understands the difference between small, rather inconsequential details that do not merit time and attention, and those lapses which should set off loud sirens and start raising big red flags. There is a vast difference between forgetting to do something, even something important, and in being dishonest or in sowing disunity. The "yeast" Jesus was speaking about is evil. He was warning about the way it contaminates when it is introduced in even small amounts. This is a powerful lesson for those in leadership.

The "yeast" of Herod and the Pharisees was a growing corruption and evil disposition that, while small at this point, would eventually spread throughout the land. Jesus could clearly see the day coming when the small clouds on the horizon would eventually become thunderheads of controversy, breaking over His head amid the lightning and thunder of the last week of His life.

It's not as if the disciples were unaware of the opposition. They had experienced the hostility themselves; but like most followers, they couldn't see where it was leading. Jesus knew because He saw the future clearly. Here He moved to warn His men of the danger they themselves would face in the future.

Some problems a leader should overlook or, at most, quietly and privately mention about the needed correction to the person responsible. However, some kinds of problems should never be overlooked, and the entire organization should know that the leader has "hit the roof" over them. Dishonesty and disunity are two of these. At the very first sign of either, the leader should move swiftly and forcefully to deal with them. Never put these on the "back burner."

They, like other kinds of evil, will only grow and contaminate the entire operation.

By "hitting the roof," we do not mean that histrionics are in order and that a leader must yell and scream when faced with a situation which must be handled. We do mean that a swift and decisive action must be taken and that, somehow, the word must be delivered that dishonesty and disloyalty, even in small doses, will not be tolerated.

The kind of "buzz" you want to create is "Did you know that Marcia is no longer with us? I guess even petty cash is not considered petty around here." Or "The boss heard that Steve has been promising customers more than we could ever hope to deliver. Steve is not with us anymore." Or "You know Kevin, who is always spouting off about how bad our company is? Evidently he was told that if it was so bad, he should find somewhere else to work."

Leaders must be able to recognize the "yeast of the Pharisees" and be willing to deal with it immediately.

CHAPTER 20

A FOCUS ON FOCUS

"Do you have eyes but fail to see, and ears but fail to hear?

And don't you remember?"

Mark 8:18

Just as the disciples focused on the relatively minor problem of having no bread and, in their concern about it, demonstrated a lack of faith—particularly in the light of the great miracle they had just witnessed—followers today often become unfocused, forget past victories, and give in to fear and uncertainty. A leader must refocus, remind, and reassure.

In every kind of endeavor, from coaching a team to building a business to running a church, the leader must guard against a lack of focus. A leader must begin this vigilance with himself or herself. When a leader loses focus, the enterprise suffers. Too often, this lack of leadership focus leads to collapse and total failure.

When a corporate chief becomes enamored with a seemingly glamorous new undertaking that has nothing to do with the company's core business, problems ensue. When church leadership begins to see increased attendance (or some other secondary goal) as its primary goal instead of making obedient disciples, real blessings are sacrificed. Leadership must remain focused, must adhere to the mission statement. If a leader loses focus, all the others involved are sure to follow.

But how does a leader keep his own focus? The first few minutes of any day are very crucial for everything that follows. Does he or she spend time dedicating the day to God and asking for His direction? What about thinking strategically about the three or four most important things you need to do that day?

Some leaders have a mission statement they paste on their dashboard or on the mirror in the bathroom at home so it will never be far from their minds. I know other leaders who have a list of questions they ask themselves every morning:

1. What things do I need to do today that no one but I can do effectively?
2. What things on my list could be better done by someone else?
3. What problems have I been putting off because I don't want to deal with them?

4. What steps—however small—could I take today that will lead my company into the future?

5. What should I do today that will make me glad when today becomes yesterday?

6. How can I encourage the people around me today in what they have to do?

Questions such as these are vital because they force the leader to think about his priorities and help him stay focused. If he loses his focus, the people around him will soon lose theirs.

Note also the strategy Jesus followed to reassure His disciples:

1. He asked six very pointed questions.

2. The questions move from the problem to the root cause (unbelief caused by a bad memory).

3. He reminded them of two amazing miracles in the recent past.

4. He challenged them with the thought that by now they should have understood all of this without any explanation.

To call this reassurance may sound strange because it seems more like rebuke, but in reality Jesus was reassuring His disciples that despite their slow learning curve, He was still willing to work with them. He was also showing them that He had greater faith in them (and higher expectations) than they had for themselves.

No doubt it was no fun to be rebuked by Jesus; but in the end, the experience did them a world of good. It's like a highly respected coach telling his team, "You can do better, and because you can do better, I'm not going to be satisfied until that's exactly what happens." It stings, but the long-term impact produces followers who eventually become leaders.

CHAPTER 21

CALCULATE YOUR ACTIONS

MARK 8:22–26

He took the blind man by the hand and led him outside the village.

Mark 8:23

It is interesting to note that Jesus sometimes did things in unexpected ways. Obviously, He could have healed the blind man on the spot, right where he stood, without so much as lifting His finger. That He did not do so provides us with a valuable leadership lesson. It is important for leaders to understand that it is not only immediate results which count, but also the long-range impact the results will have. Sometimes it will be necessary to accomplish something "outside the villages" to achieve maximum positive impact. Too, the easiest way to get something done may not always be the best way to get it done.

This is the only place in the Gospels where Jesus healed in stages. Understanding why is made more difficult because the text doesn't clearly explain itself. Some obvious applications are:

1. Jesus does indeed have the power to open blinded eyes.
2. He has the power to heal instantly or in stages.
3. Jesus involved Himself in a very personal way in this man's problems.
4. He solved the problem in a way that also taught a lesson to His disciples.

Most commentators think that Jesus was teaching His disciples that they were like the blind man who had been partially healed. They saw Jesus dimly—not clearly—and they needed greater illumination from the Holy Spirit in order for their spiritual vision to clear.

Leaders of today, too, shouldn't be shocked that their followers are slow to grab the big picture. They must repeatedly and intentionally find moments when they can "teach by example" the overall mission of the organization.

It's worth noting that Jesus is here responding to a need of the moment. The man's friends brought him to Jesus. Healing a blind man wasn't on the day's agenda—speaking from a purely human point of view—but Jesus understood that this "interruption" actually provided a powerful moment for demonstrating His power, His compassion, and His commitment to His overall mission. He was "on task" even though the incident might have seemed like a distraction.

Incidentally, note that Jesus instructed the man not to go back into town. This, of course, would be the first place he wanted to go. This suggests that the miracle was being done not so much for public consumption but for the benefit of the disciples.

Wise leaders, like Jesus, will calculate their actions to produce the greatest good and to teach the most powerful lessons.

CHAPTER 22

ON THE ROAD AGAIN

Jesus and his disciples went on to the villages around Caesarea Philippi.

On the way he asked them, "Who do people say I am?"

Mark 8:27

This passage is full of lessons leaders need to learn. Perhaps the first is that a leader must be willing to go where the action is, must be willing to take the tough road trip. Jesus was headquartered in Capernaum, but we most often encounter Him on the road. And Caesarea Philippi was a particularly pagan city, a Greek city of some note in the first century.

Caesarea Philippi originally was a Canaanite center of Baal worship. Later it was named after the Greek god Pan. Still later Herod built a temple there in honor of Caesar Augustus. Finally Herod Phillip (a different Herod) expanded the city and renamed it after himself and the emperor Tiberius Caesar. Thus there was a strong Roman-Greek flavor to the town and an even stronger commitment to pagan worship. In spirit it was far removed from the cities and towns of Israel. Here Jesus was truly on "foreign soil."

Jesus did not just send His disciples into this tough area to pass out brochures; He led them into it. A quality leader often leads his troops into battle, he doesn't always just send them. As you lead, be alert for those occasions when the cause is best served by your presence. One corporate leader I know has a sort of rule of thumb which says, "The trip I want least to take is probably the one I should be certain to make."

A wise leader takes the tough trip with followers. On almost all occasions, Jesus traveled with His disciples and used the travel time to teach.

As we worked to build our company over three decades, some of the most profitable and rewarding times were spent traveling with our younger colleagues. I credit my partner with the wisdom of suggesting that even when the two of us were on the same plane, we should spend some of the flying hours with one of our younger associates. Those people are now in key positions. Jesus demonstrated this leadership lesson over and over.

CHAPTER 23

THE DISCIPLES' FINAL EXAM
MARK 8:27–30

"But what about you?" he asked. "Who do you say I am?"

Mark 8:29

The film *The Bridge on the River Kwai* was one of the most compelling of all World War II motion pictures. In very dramatic fashion it tells a story which illustrates how easy it is for even the most intelligent and dedicated to become so focused on a secondary objective that the primary overarching goal is forgotten. In the film, the ranking British officer in a group of soldiers captured by the Japanese becomes so intent on using the building of a bridge as a way to maintain discipline and esprit de corps among his men that he forgets the reason they are there in the first place: to defeat the Japanese. A completed bridge will be a huge asset to the Japanese war effort. But because he has lost sight of the extremely important primary mission, he goes to even heroic efforts to build the bridge, thereby aiding the enemy.

A continuing theme of John MacArthur, noted pastor and Bible teacher, is how easy it is for the church to become distracted and to lose sight of its mission. Loss of focus causes even once-great churches to become insignificant. When this happens, so-called outreach committees focus on such trivia as ushers! No thought is given to the unchurched of the community except to work on how they would be directed to their seats should they happen to wander into the sanctuary! After creating order and insisting on unity, maintaining focus is the order of the day, every day, for leaders.

When Jesus asked the question in the key verse, He knew that before long He would hang on a cross. But before He could do that, He had to know where His men stood. He had to bring them out in the open. Were they with Him? Did they know who He really was? If you want to think of it in school terms, this was the disciples' final exam.

This time Jesus received a marvelous, thrilling answer from Peter. Often before, the answers to similar questions had told Him He had more teaching to do.

Jesus was one of the earliest proponents of public opinion research. In His question, He was gauging the impact of His message and His mission. It is very important for a leader not to lose touch with the people most affected by his or her leadership. To do this, a leader must have a close core of followers who have the confidence to tell him or her the truth.

Some leaders, early on, signal that they will tolerate only good news. This is a terrible mistake. The most valuable follower a leader can have is one who will deliver the tough truth. When a leader asks, "How am I doing?" (and this is a question that should be asked periodically), a trusted and trusting follower should be able and willing to give a truthful, unvarnished answer.

Be sure you engender this kind of trust in a group of close associates who will be willing to give you both the good news and the bad news, both about how you are doing and about how people perceive your leadership effectiveness. Use their truthful, honest answers to make your future leadership more effective.

CHAPTER 24

TRUE CONFESSION

"But what about you?" he asked. "Who do you say I am?"

Peter answered, "You are the Christ."

Mark 8:29

"Who do you say I am?" In the Greek text, that word *you* has an enormous stress. In fact, the *you* really goes at the first of the sentence. It is as if Jesus is saying, "But you who have followed Me and have known Me from the beginning, who do *you* say I am?" *It is the greatest question in all the universe, and it is one which every person must eventually answer.*

Peter answers for all the disciples. That's because he was the D. L. — the Designated Loudmouth. Whenever there was a question, Peter would always be the first one to answer. And when Peter answers here, he is not speaking simply for himself, but for all the disciples.

His answer is very, very specific: "You are the Christ." Peter was saying, "I know who You are. You are the Messiah sent to save us, and You are the Son of God from heaven." It is short and simple. Everything necessary for salvation is included in that statement.

Note that Peter said, "You are the Christ." Not "I say You are the Christ" or "People say You are the Christ" or even "We got together and took a vote and we think You are the Christ." It is a declarative statement—"You are the Christ."

Some people would read that statement and say, "Well, that's no big deal. I would say that, too." Most Christians would probably stand up and say, "You are the Christ." But Peter was the first person in human history ever to say it out loud. And he said it when few were with Jesus and many were against Him. He deserves all the credit, for without his confession there would be no Christian church. In that sense, there is a direct line between Caesarea Philippi and the Christian movement at the end of the twentieth century. We would not be here if Peter had not opened his mouth.

A leader must earn the kind of affirmation Peter gave to Jesus. Earning it, not expecting it or demanding it, should be every leader's goal.

Leadership can be charted, analyzed, managed, ordered, and, to some extent, manufactured. But in its most powerful and important manifestation, it must be personal, emotive, and, to some extent, spontaneous. The carefully drawn organizational charts only have life and real meaning to the extent that, at key points, followers are saying to leaders, "I *will* follow *you*."

When this response comes, it is electrifying, energizing, and unifying. Leader and follower come together in a binding way, sealed together in a commitment to accomplish a worthwhile objective. This kind of bond is the most rewarding part of leadership and helps to make all the heavy costs of leadership worthwhile.

A leader earns the right to this special kind of relationship through an active involvement with his or her people. It is earned when care and concern are demonstrated. It is earned by accepting at least some of the same rigors followers are expected to undergo.

Be the kind of leader who earns the kind of affirmation that produces results.

CHAPTER 25

HOW TO DISPENSE NEWS

Jesus warned them not to tell anyone about him.

Mark 8:30

Obviously, Jesus wanted everyone to know who He was. He came to earth and invaded space and time "that they might know." He left behind all the glory that was His as a member of the Godhead so that men and women would come to *know* Him. He would suffer death, "even death on a cross," for the very reason that people should know Him and why He came. With all this in mind, the verse above becomes a tremendously powerful leadership lesson. When it is coupled with all the other instances cited in Mark and the other Gospels in which Jesus instructed both His disciples and others *not* to tell, we have a lesson for leaders not to be missed.

What seems to be an obvious non sequitur—Jesus' desire that all should know Him, and His many instructions not to tell, makes sense only when we understand that the timing, location, and method of releasing information determines its ultimate impact. The wisest leaders understand that information, like authority, is one of the basic tools of leadership. By virtue of position, a leader will have access to information that no one else will have. How and when that information is used will play a major role in determining the effectiveness of leaders.

Why did Jesus repeatedly tell His followers not to tell anyone else about Him? It boils down to two realities. First, His followers weren't ready for the news to be released. Even His inner circle still didn't have a full understanding of why He had come. Consider that just moments after Peter's amazing declaration of faith, Jesus rebuked him and said, "Get behind me, Satan!" Essentially, Peter clearly understood *who* Jesus was, but still didn't fully grasp *why* He had come.

In fact, the disciples would be in the dark regarding the crucifixion right up to the last moments of Jesus' life. They never really understood that Jesus *had* to die until after it happened. Jesus couldn't risk having the message go out publicly until His own key men fully grasped both His true identity and the mission God had given Him.

Second, the people of Israel weren't expecting a suffering Messiah. They were looking for a political/spiritual leader who could free them from Roman rule. If too many reports of His miracles were spread abroad, it might ignite a political movement that would divert Jesus from His mission as Savior of the world.

Did Jesus "manage" the news regarding who He was and why He came? Absolutely. To do otherwise was to risk ruining everything He came to do. At this critical point in His ministry, neither His key leaders nor the public at large were ready for the "good news" to be announced. That time would come. Jesus knew it, and He steadily moved toward that day. Until that day came, He steadfastly refused unnecessary publicity.

It is important to say here that in managing information, truth is never compromised or manipulated. Jesus never lied, never distorted the truth. Good leadership *always* is truthful leadership. It is how and when truth is used which is the subject of this lesson.

"Need to know" is one method leaders use to manage information. Important information is released primarily only to those persons and only at the time that they really *need* it, in order to advance the enterprise. A pastor and church leaders may be contemplating a very necessary move to new church facilities. To release that information to the total congregation before important decisions are made about the relocation would probably sow confusion and unnecessary concern. An effective leader will assess when that time has come.

In corporate life, a leader will often know well in advance when layoffs will be coming. How and when that information is released will determine how it impacts both the enterprise and individual lives. A wise and compassionate leader will balance those in the best way possible. He will make these kinds of decisions the subject of much prayer.

Jesus came to bring good news, the best of all possible news. The way He managed its "release" should be instructive to all leaders. Good news, good information, like bad, needs to be managed so that it will produce the greatest possible good. Jesus knew that necessary groundwork must be laid before the good news was declared for all to hear. He knew that timing was all-important. He had a plan that included when and how the news was to be made known to all. Effective leaders will never dispense information in a haphazard way.

One of the leadership lessons the life of Jesus teaches is that good news is most powerful when it is not dribbled out, but when it is released in a major way, at an important time to the right group of people. To manage news and information most effectively, it is important not to hold it too long. When leaks occur, even benign leaks, the news begins to manage you, as you must react and respond to it rather than the other way around.

Jesus used information very carefully. He managed it. Its use was an important and integral part of His plan. These are vital lessons for all leaders.

CHAPTER 26

PREPARING FOR THE HARD TIMES

He then began to teach them that the Son of Man must suffer many things

and be rejected by the elders, chief priests and teachers of the law, and

that he must be killed and after three days rise again.

Mark 8:31

Jesus began to prepare His disciples for the extremely difficult days ahead only after Peter's great affirmation, "You are the Christ." They had begun to grasp the good news about who Jesus was and why He came. Now they would need to understand the cost involved, the price to be paid, to be a part of Christ's mission. At this point, they had witnessed the healings, the miracles of feeding the masses, the casting out of demons, and even the control over weather. They had experienced the heady occasions when their Master had bounced around the haughty Pharisees by the power of His words. Now it was necessary for them to be prepared for the inevitable tough times.

Inevitable is a key word here. Wise leaders will understand that in every human endeavor of any scope or magnitude, there will be tough times. Difficulties *will* occur. The best leaders do all they can to prepare followers for these times of stress. Followers should never be taken by surprise by difficulties. As much as possible, surprises should always be on the "upside." Followers should not be able to say to a leader, "You never told us it would be like this."

As we examine the leadership of Jesus, we see that He very clearly and forcefully laid out the great promise of His mission: "I will make you fishers of men." Now it was necessary to lay out the great costs involved: "The Son of Man must suffer many things. . . ."

Consider the little word *must*. Behind it stands the full weight of all the prophecies of the Old Testament regarding the coming of our Lord. The word *must* reminds us that nothing that happened to Jesus happened by chance. All was predicted and foreordained by God's gracious plan. But this "must" leads on to suffering, pain, humiliation, and death. Can that be God's plan? Indeed it can and is—not just for Jesus, but for all of us.

There is much that might be said at this point regarding a proper theology of suffering. But this much is always true: God allows suffering to come to His children—to all of them sooner or later. Although salvation is free, the road to heaven is paved with "many dangers, toils, and snares."

Notice also that Jesus was very specific at this point. He would "suffer . . . be rejected . . . by the elders, chief priests and teachers of the law . . . he must be killed." The very specificity no doubt weighed heavily on the minds of the disciples. It's one thing to say, "I've got a bad feeling in the pit of my stomach." It's something else to say, "At 4 P.M. on Friday I'm going to be electrocuted." The fact that Jesus could state these things reveals something about His mastery of the circumstances and His confidence in His disciples. Even though they didn't fully grasp what He was saying, He "began" to unravel the dark side of the future.

Finally, Jesus also mentioned the resurrection—a fact the disciples grasped even less than His crucifixion. Since they really couldn't believe He would be killed, they seemed not to have understood the resurrection at all. But the bare mention of the resurrection was a way of giving ultimate hope to His followers: "Here's the light at the end of the tunnel." It's truly a dark tunnel, but what a light that shines from the empty tomb!

Followers should know about the risk/reward ratio. The greater the risk, the greater the reward. They should also know that risks cannot be avoided, so it is not foolish to take risks in a great and exciting cause. As Jim Elliot, the great missionary martyr, said, "He is no fool who gives what he cannot keep to gain what he cannot lose." Leaders of today need to be articulating both messages in cogent and powerful ways.

As leaders follow the example of Jesus, they will teach about and demonstrate the exciting possibilities of the effort to which they are committed. Followers and potential followers will get a realistic look at the upside, the rewards of success. This should motivate and excite them. However, a leader for the long haul will also, at the right time, clearly lay out the costs necessary to obtain that success: "For us to make it, all of us will have to put in a lot of hard work. There will be long hours and a great deal of travel involved. It will not be easy." Even the possibility of ultimate failure should be touched upon. "You know, no one has ever attempted this before. Even with our best efforts, we might not succeed" are statements to be considered.

I know all about the philosophy that says, "We will not even consider failure. We won't allow it to happen." That looks good as a slogan on a locker room wall, but it is not realistic in real life, in real human endeavors. No leader plans to fail, but many do. Almost all do at one point or another. The best and wisest prepare followers for this while leading and motivating toward success.

Jesus taught about both success and failure. He laid out the rewards to be obtained and the cost involved in obtaining them. He made sure there would be a minimum of unpleasant surprises. Great leadership!

CHAPTER 27

TOUGH LOVE

But when Jesus turned and looked at his disciples, he rebuked Peter.

"Get behind me, Satan!" he said. "You do not have in mind the things of

God, but the things of men."

Mark 8:33

In our "seeker-sensitive," politically correct world, where building a person's self-esteem is held to be a teacher's and a leader's highest goal, even the word *rebuke* seems archaic. Modern management and leadership theory would not support the kind of powerful, devastating rebuke Jesus gave Peter. This was no namby-pamby invitation to "sit down and talk this over" or to "see how we can reach consensus on this." It was no "I'm okay. You're okay" kind of transaction. This was a very pointed, forcefully delivered, scathing reprimand. The exclamation Mark included in the Scripture is there to show that this was a forceful pronouncement. And it was delivered in public. No one's feelings were spared with this one. A rebuke, even a stinging one, is a potent and valuable leadership device.

It is important to look at Jesus' rebuke of Peter in some detail. Perhaps the most important thing to note is its rarity. This kind of rebuke, far from representing a pattern of Jesus' leadership, was singular. This added to its great effect.

I know a corporate leader who is constantly, daily delivering rebukes of the magnitude and intensity of the one we are considering here. They have long since lost much of their positive impact. People get tired of them and begin to look for other jobs.

On the other hand, I played college basketball for a coach of the mildest manner. He almost never raised his voice. But on occasion, when our team had lost concentration and discipline, he really let us have it. His one rebuke was effective for an entire year! Those of us who were subjected to it still talk about it forty years later. The lesson is obvious: Use a strong rebuke rarely.

Secondly, it is important to be discerning about the person receiving the rebuke. Peter—bold, brash, and self-confident—could receive the rebuke and, while certainly stung, could rebound and come back stronger than ever from such a scolding. Jesus didn't deliver the rebuke to destroy Peter, but to build him up. However, this kind of rebuke might have destroyed John, a much more sensitive disciple.

Reserve your sharpest rebukes for your strongest followers. Use them to build up, not to tear down.

Too, use them where they will have a positive effect beyond the person to whom they are directed. The Scripture says, "But when Jesus turned and looked at his disciples, he rebuked Peter." He rebuked Peter, but the lesson was obviously for the entire group. You can be sure that all the disciples learned a great deal from the rebuke directed at Peter.

One of the most important and powerful lessons here is that, as a leader, Jesus demonstrated that none of His followers were beyond reproof and correction. Even Peter, who received Jesus' great affirmation, was still a follower subject to being taught by the leader. In all kinds of endeavors, those closest to the leader are sometimes those most in need of a rebuke, even a public one. They sometimes need "to be brought up short." When they are not, bad things happen, things that could have been prevented by a well-timed, well-placed rebuke.

A gifted and experienced elementary school teacher recalled the days when misbehaving students were routinely paddled—sometimes in front of the class, more often in the hallway. Why in the hallway? Because the sound of the paddling could be heard in many other classrooms. The teacher spoke of the hush that fell on the other students when he was giving some miscreant three whacks on the rear end. "I could paddle one boy and make three hundred others sit up straight," he said. Rebukes when done appropriately benefit many others besides the one being disciplined.

Why did Peter speak as he did to Jesus? Verse 32 says that Jesus was speaking "plainly" about His coming sufferings. Perhaps Peter felt He was being a bit too bold, too honest, too forthright. Maybe he thought that Jesus would only discourage the other men. He probably thought to himself, *I can handle this, but Thomas won't like it and Simon the Zealot will want to start a riot in Jerusalem. Better tell Jesus to lay off all this death talk for a while.* What's more, Peter handled the situation appropriately. He took Jesus aside and spoke to Him privately—which is exactly how a subordinate should speak to a leader in this situation.

That's what makes Jesus' rebuke so unexpected. I'm sure it blew Peter away. It seemed almost unfair and unkind. And it would be—unless truly important issues are at stake. If Peter had had his way, Jesus' mission would not have been accomplished; His whole purpose for coming to earth would have been foiled.

This shows how easily a key leader can—with good intentions—miss the larger picture and throw the whole organization off course. Jesus *had* to do what He did, hurt feelings or not, and not just for Peter's sake, but for all His men—who were probably thinking the same thing but were afraid to say it.

Finally, consider the phrase "Get behind me, Satan." It seems incredibly harsh—and even cruel. But Peter was really repeating (unwittingly) Satan's earlier attempt in the wilderness to distract Jesus from His mission of salvation. By calling Peter "Satan," Jesus indicated the source of Peter's wrong ideas and in a sense pointed the way toward forgiveness and restoration. "Peter, don't you see that I *must* die. If you oppose that, you are actually doing Satan's work. And if you want to follow Me, you must know that I will end up on the cross. There is no other way."

Suppose Jesus had said, "Get behind Me, Peter." That would have been a thousand times worse because it would be a personal rejection of the man—not simply of his misguided ideas. So there is grace hidden beneath this very stinging rebuke.

A strong public rebuke should never be given for anything but the most important of reasons. Jesus' rebuke of Peter was given only when the very core of His mission was threatened by Peter. A very pointed, very direct, not-to-be misunderstood rebuke was in order. Jesus delivered it.

Among the most important leadership lessons is that Jesus had "earned" the right to deliver a rebuke. Jesus had demonstrated His care for Peter from the time He gave him a personal call to follow, to the healing of his mother-in-law, to allowing him to witness many miracles, to singling him out for special teaching. Peter had to know that Jesus loved him and that even this kind of rebuke was delivered in love. Tough love, maybe, but love nevertheless.

As we lead, and as the need to rebuke presents itself, we need to be sure we have "earned" the right to deliver it. Our leadership should be of sufficient duration that both our commitment to the mission and our care for our followers have been clearly demonstrated. Only then should we consider the kind of rebuke Jesus gave Peter.

Even with all the conditions, considerations, and caveats, leaders should never forget the importance of a rebuke. It might not be a politically correct leadership technique, but it is an effective one. Jesus demonstrated this, and He is the greatest leader of all time.

CHAPTER 28

SPEAKING TO INSPIRE
MARK 8:31–38

Then he called the crowd to him along with his disciples and said:

"If anyone would come after me, he must deny himself and take up his

cross and follow me."

Mark 8:34

Too many leaders neglect the art of inspiring, challenging public speaking. This is a mistake because public speaking is a skill that everyone can develop. Practice, work, and determination can make any leader a better speaker and, thereby, a more effective leader.

Jesus used public speaking as one of His primary leadership tools. He spoke to instruct—as in the Sermon on the Mount and when He called the crowd to Him to teach about clean and unclean things—and to inspire and challenge—as in the passage cited here. He was a masterful public speaker. Leaders down through the ages have profited from His example. Abraham Lincoln, perhaps the most effective of American political speakers, is said to have modeled his speaking on the discourses of Jesus. Leaders today should do the same.

Note that Jesus' stinging rebuke of Peter, while done in the presence of the disciples, was *not* done before the general public—who wouldn't have understood it anyway. Also, Jesus' timing is obviously critical. He first secures an understanding from His key men regarding who He is. Only then does He lay out the suffering that is to come. And only after that does He rebuke Peter. Those were all "inside" tasks that had to be completed first.

Note the method Jesus used to gather the crowd's attention. He begins with the fact of His own popularity with the masses: "If anyone would come after me." That only makes sense if people were already attracted to His cause. But what will He ask for? Self-denial and the way of death.

"Take up your cross" has become a kind of proverb in Christian circles, so much so that we forget how radical it must have sounded in the first century. The cross was an instrument of Roman torture. At times the roads around Jerusalem were lined with hundreds of crosses bearing dead and dying men, their bodies bloated in the sun, surrounded by flies, covered with maggots. It's not a pretty thought or one calculated to win the masses. Yet that's the image Jesus calls to mind.

In Jesus' day, condemned criminals were made to carry the crossbar to the place of their own execution. Here Jesus is calling men to come and die in His service. We forget the shock of His words. He was calling His followers to heroic effort in the face of certain opposition, suffering, pain, and death. Not everyone would be willing to pay the price. By putting the matter so boldly, Jesus is "making the first cut" up front.

Great speakers understand that people respond to a great challenge—even one involving huge personal sacrifice when (1) they believe in the person making the challenge, (2) they see the challenge itself as being worthwhile, and (3) the challenge isn't sugarcoated but is put in stark, unforgettable terms. Too many public speakers mumble and drone when they would be far more effective if they said less and said it in a simple, direct way.

One of the most effective ways to become a better public speaker is to have someone you trust critique your speeches. Be sure this is someone who is not a "yes man," but someone you can count on to give you honest feedback. Jesus didn't need a critique. He *knew* how effective He was. None of us can be as sure.

Be a challenging, inspiring public speaker. It is a skill worth developing. Model your presentations after those of Jesus.

CHAPTER 29

CULTIVATING LOYALTY

"If anyone is ashamed of me and my words in this adulterous and sinful

generation, the Son of Man will be ashamed of him when he comes in his

Father's glory with the holy angels."

Mark 8:38

It's interesting to consider the background of this verse. From the disciples' point of view, there were many reasons to be ashamed of Jesus. First of all, He lacked the support of the religious/political establishment and was therefore an "outsider." Instead of leading a popular uprising, He set forth a spiritual kingdom that demanded things such as self-denial and taking up the cross—an abhorrent thought to first-century Jews. And Jesus Himself has just predicted His own suffering and eventual death—factors not likely to increase His public popularity. So these words are far from hyperbole.

As a good leader, Jesus knew that it would be easy for His men to give up and simply walk away. But note the promise implicit in His words: Those who stay with Me will share with Me when I gain the final victory at the end of time.

Finally, consider how personal this appeal is. If you are "ashamed" of Me, I will be "ashamed" of you. This speaks of the tight bond that exists between the best leaders and their followers. In the end, great leaders call forth such deeply personal loyalty that a man would rather die than cause his hero to be ashamed of him. This is the kind of challenge that caused the men at the Alamo to die for Texas and more than nine hundred Jews to commit suicide at Masada. Better to die for the cause than to live in shame.

Loyalty, like unity, with which it is closely allied, is a leadership absolute, an imperative. It is something that a leader should expect and on which he should be able to rely. Without loyalty, there really is no leader/follower relationship. A leader must cultivate and reward loyalty and must punish and expel those who are disloyal. This may seem harsh, but it is a leadership lesson of Jesus.

Loyalty does not mean mindless, uncritical devotion. That is worship, and no one other than Jesus is worthy of worship. Leaders make a grave mistake when they exercise the kind of leadership which requires any kind of submission. When this happens, leadership has degenerated into paranoia. This is not loyalty.

Loyalty is exercised primarily outside the group. Sometimes the most loyal thing a follower can do is to openly disagree with a leader. Because he cares about both the leader and the mission, he is willing to say, "Wait a minute. I think we are making a mistake here. Please explain to me why this is the best policy." These kinds of questions, openly asked of a leader, do not represent disloyalty. A wise leader should be open to answering honest questions and to dealing with honest disagreements. This builds and sustains both loyalty and unity.

Disloyalty occurs within the group when questions and disagreements are not openly asked and openly discussed. This sows disunity and must be curtailed. An even more serious kind of disloyalty occurs when followers do not support the leader and the mission outside the group, especially among the competition or opposition. This is the kind of thing Jesus was warning about in this passage. When a follower is disloyal and denigrates the leader or the endeavor outside the group, he is, in actuality, no longer a follower and should not be treated as such. Unless and until the disloyalty is dealt with and the person restored (as was the case with Peter later on), he should be expelled from the group.

A leader cannot and should not tolerate disloyalty. Jesus didn't.

CHAPTER 30

BOLD LEADERSHIP

And he said to them, "I tell you the truth, some who are standing here will

not taste death before they see the kingdom of God come with power."

Mark 9:1

The specific event predicted here evidently is the transfiguration, which occurred six days later. Here is a case where Jesus knew something His disciples would not have foreseen. They had no reason to expect that an event like the transfiguration was about to occur. Most likely they interpreted Jesus' comments to be a reference to the final setting up of the kingdom of God on the earth.

The timing is important. In the preceding verses we have Peter's confession, Peter's rebuke by Jesus, the challenge of cross-bearing, the call to total commitment, and the challenge of personal loyalty. The way is now cleared, so to speak, for the final portion of Jesus' public ministry. In racing terms, Jesus is now making the final turn into the homestretch. As He does so, He offers (via the transfiguration) a glimpse of His ultimate glory when He returns as King over all the earth. That vital experience will be increasingly important as the opposition grows and as the final days of Jesus' life are played out amid controversy, suffering, and death.

So we can say that Jesus, knowing what the future would hold, picks an opportune moment to make a bold statement—which His men wouldn't immediately understand—that leads to an experience which would prepare them emotionally for the hard times to come.

The most powerful and effective leadership is bold leadership. It is not rash. It does not promise what it cannot deliver. It does not go in for "grandstand plays," those showy performances which serve primarily to build personal ego. Just as Jesus used this occasion to make a bold and powerful assertion, wise leaders will look for occasions when they can make their own prudent, but potent and provocative statements.

Dave Dixon, the imaginative and innovative sports entrepreneur, made two of the boldest statements ever made in American sports. The first was that we were going to build the greatest sports stadium in the world. We did, the Superdome in New Orleans. The second was, in some ways, even bolder. I was visiting his home in New Orleans and, out of the blue, he turned to me and said, "Bob, you and I are going to take over tennis and turn it into a major spectator sport worldwide." Sure, Dave. Neither of us had ever even seen an official tennis match, but Dave Dixon was the kind of bold leader who turned bold statements into bold reality. In fact, we did take over tennis; and the $100 million-plus worldwide professional tennis circuit is the result of what we did. A bold leader makes calculated, bold statements which motivate and energize followers into making them come true.

As bold as He was, Jesus never promised more than He could and would deliver. In this, and in all things, He should be our pattern.

CHAPTER 31

WHY INTIMACY IS IMPORTANT

MARK 9:2–8

After six days Jesus took Peter, James and John with him and led them

up a high mountain, where they were all alone. There he was

transfigured before them.

Mark 9:2

Mark doesn't tell us why Jesus singled out James, Peter, and John to go with Him to the mountain. They definitely seem to have been part of His inner circle from the earliest days of His ministry. They were among His first followers, were present at some miracles the others did not witness, and were always mentioned first in every listing of the apostles. This suggests that Jesus established a close relationship with these three from the very beginning—a relationship the rest of the disciples acknowledged, even if they did not fully understand.

Note that Jesus apparently makes no explanation as to why these three men are chosen and others are not. Certainly He saw them as representative of the others and knew they would tell the others what they had experienced. By this point in Jesus' ministry, the other nine men knew that James, Peter, and John had an intimate relationship with the Lord; so no explanation was needed. In any case, no leader can ever fully explain why he is drawn to one person and not to another. In most cases, it's better not to try to explain it.

More leadership has failed from a lack of intimacy than from any other cause. Leaders, no matter how brilliant, cut their tenures short or accomplish less than they might otherwise when they fail to establish close relationships with a few key people, a core of their followers. I have been in situations where followers, including myself, sought a closer relationship with a leader, not for personal gain, but for his sake and for the sake of the enterprise—only to be rebuffed. Every time a leader tries to "go it alone," something less than the best occurs.

The very nature of leadership requires some distance between a leader and the bulk of his or her followers. It is impossible to lead and to be close with everyone. However, the very nature of leadership also requires a close, intimate relationship characterized by a degree of vulnerability with at least *some* followers. Too, the more demanding, complex, and stressful the undertaking, the more a closeness with an inner core becomes necessary. Certainly a church, a school, a team, and almost all business endeavors require that a leader develop an intimacy with a core group in order to *produce* maximum success for all concerned. To accept the cliché "It is lonely at the top" is to accept a leadership style which will deliver less than it should.

Pastors, even those in large churches, are among the leaders who find it most difficult to establish a close, honest, caring relationship with an inner core of believers. In some cases, the more gifted a pastor is in the preaching ministry, the more possibility there is that he will increasingly isolate himself from others. This is a recipe for difficulty and sometimes for tragedy. Of all leaders, pastors are most in need of the kind of fellowship, support, and honest criticism they can receive from a small inner circle. For a look at the positive side of this, I suggest *Unveiled Hope* by Scotty Smith and Michael Card, which details how the dynamic Christ Community Church in Franklin, Tennessee, was built on the ideal of intimacy and accountability.

Leaders who fear intimacy will look for all kinds of excuses to avoid it. One of the most common, particularly in the church, is: "I can't be seen showing favoritism by getting too close to any one group of people. I must treat everyone the same." This is not only nonsense; it is not scriptural.

The results of Jesus' investment in a particularly close relationship with Peter, James, and John are very evident. James was the first disciple put to death for his commitment to Jesus. John went on to write his Gospel, three letters, and the marvelous Book of Revelation. And of course Peter, along with Paul, became a most important leader of the church. All the disciples would eventually become leaders in the early church, but these three would be in the first rank. Jesus knew that and chose them to share in the intimate transfiguration experience with Him.

Leaders must develop a core group of followers in whom they confide and from whom they expect honest feedback and wholehearted support. Building this core may not be easy. There may be fits and starts. Some chosen for it may not themselves be ready for the kind of relationship it requires. There may be some pain involved. Regardless, it is well worth it. In fact, quality long-term leadership is not possible without it.

CHAPTER 32

THE POWER OF OUTSIDE AFFIRMATIONS

Then a cloud appeared and enveloped them, and a voice came from the

cloud: "This is my Son, whom I love. Listen to him!"

Mark 9:7

Jesus had a special reason for taking Peter, James, and John with Him to witness the transfiguration and to hear the voice from the cloud. Jesus was continually giving them a basis to believe the amazing things He was telling them. Particularly, He was preparing them for the excruciating times which were now looming close. It was a good thing He did. Even with all the miracles performed in their presence, even with all the brilliant teaching conducted in their hearing, and even with this awesome, transcendent experience of the transfiguration, their belief flickered and went out or, at least, burned very low at the time of the arrest and crucifixion.

Evidently the transfiguration made a huge impact on Peter, who mentioned this event some thirty years later near the end of his life. In 2 Peter 1:16–18 Peter recalls this momentous event and uses it to argue for the truth of the gospel. He *knows* the gospel is true because he heard the voice from heaven—a voice he could never forget. Therefore (he is arguing), his words can be trusted because he was there as an eyewitness on the mountain. He saw what happened; he heard God's voice. It's all as real to him as an old man as it was the day he first heard it.

This is *exactly* why Jesus took Peter up to the mountain in the first place. He wanted Peter to never forget that moment—and he never did. This is great leadership: a perfect sense of timing and the creation of an impression that would last long after the leader had left the scene.

Without self-aggrandizement or for ego's sake, a leader needs to build his stature among his followers. This needs to be done primarily by an obvious commitment to them and their shared mission. However, a wise leader will also look for opportunities to have outside sources confirm his worth to followers.

When a leader is asked to speak to an outside group, it is important to take along at least one or two followers so they can see the esteem in which their leader is held by those outside the group. Just as Peter, James, and John must have done, they will pass on what they have seen and heard to other followers. If a leader is given a significant honor, such as an industry award or an honorary doctorate, this is a great opportunity to have followers present and, if possible, to participate.

One of the most important reasons for a leader to submit to media interviews and to accept outside writing assignments is to enable followers to read or hear what is written or said. A most important audience is the one inside the organization. "Hey, did you see what the *Times* said about the boss?" or "Did you catch the chief on TV last night?" are the kinds of comments that help to cement a leader's place among his or her followers.

As with everything, balance and discernment is necessary. A leader does not want to be seen as a "publicity hound." But in thoughtful, measured ways, and with the goal of strengthening leadership and advancing the cause, outside affirming exposure is valuable.

Obviously, Jesus was the furthest thing possible from an egomaniac. Yet He made sure He did not go through the transfiguration experience alone. He did not want it "wasted" as a teaching experience for His followers. This is an important lesson for every leader to learn.

CHAPTER 33

LINGERING ON THE MOUNTAINTOP

Peter said to Jesus, "Rabbi, it is good for us to be here. Let us put up

three shelters—one for you, one for Moses and one for Elijah."

Mark 9:5

Like Peter, wouldn't we all rather stay up on the mountain and enjoy the presence of the Lord? In Peter's defense, who wouldn't want to stay awhile when such amazing things are happening?

Think about the setting. They are up on the mountain when suddenly Peter sees Jesus radically and wonderfully transfigured. Then suddenly out of nowhere, Moses and Elijah show up. Hey, what are those two guys doing here? Evidently their presence serves to confirm that Jesus is indeed the promised Old Testament Messiah. They didn't appear for Jesus' sake, but for the sake of James, Peter, and John.

Peter's response is understandable in light of what was happening. He literally didn't have a clue as to what it all meant, but his first statement is certainly true—"It is good for us to be here." Most commentators suggest that Peter's idea of the shelters was an unspoken attempt to enjoy the glory of Christ without the sufferings that must precede it. We might say that his impulse was understandable but clearly wrong because Jesus had already told them that His suffering must precede His coming in glory.

There is always a time to work, and then there is a time to enjoy the fruits of your labor. First the cross, then the resurrection, is always God's pattern. That order can never be reversed. Peter had a very hard time accepting the reality that his Master would have to die, so he found every possible reason to avoid that awful moment. It was a misguided sense of love and loyalty that caused him to do these things, which is why Jesus even in His severe rebukes never rejects Peter but constantly points him back to the mission. This means enjoying the mountain while you are there, but understanding that eventually you must go back into the valley where the cross awaits.

Success and prosperity affect different people in different ways. For some, success only whets the appetite and is energizing. For others, success produces self-satisfaction and a debilitating complacency. Real leaders, particularly those in the church, are not there to manage the status quo but to lead to new heights and new victories.

Unfortunately, it is in the church where this seems to be the most difficult. In no other segment of society is complacency a bigger problem. Across the church in America the most intense current discussions are about worship styles! They should be about reaching the lost, being "salt," or making disciples. This is the current version of "Let us put up three shelters. . . ." Vigorous, robust leaders, the kind Jesus models for us, never give in to this kind of complacency, but either jump-start the situation and get it moving or move on themselves. While watching for complacency in followers, leaders must also watch carefully for it in themselves.

As Jesus led the disciples down from the mountain, He taught them and further equipped them for the job ahead. The awesome magnificence of the transfiguration provided the ultimate teachable moment. Jesus took full advantage of it. He made sure the three knew that this was the time to move. He, Jesus, was there; and He was all they needed to get on with the task at hand.

This is real leadership. Today's leaders, particularly those in the church, need to help followers understand that *today* is the day of salvation. Not only has John the Baptist already come; Jesus has already come and accomplished His mighty work, and the Holy Spirit has already come, bringing power and direction. This is no time to build three shelters and sit down. This is a time to move in faith, with vigor and determination.

CHAPTER 34

CONTROL THE FLOW OF INFORMATION

MARK 9:2–12

As they were coming down the mountain, Jesus gave them orders not to

tell anyone what they had seen until the Son of Man had risen from the

dead. They kept the matter to themselves, discussing what

"rising from the dead" meant.

Mark 9:9–10

The disciples couldn't figure out what "rising from the dead" meant. To us it seems simple, but that's because we live on this side of the empty tomb. And we accept it by faith. None of us have ever physically seen a person rise from the dead. The disciples were clueless, perhaps wondering if Jesus was referring to some general resurrection from the dead at the end of history or if the phrase meant some kind of "spiritual resurrection." At this point they simply had no way to grasp

Jesus' personal death and His physical, bodily resurrection—even though He had clearly predicted both events.

Some things simply can't be understood until they are put in proper context. The transfiguration, at the time, seemed like an amazing event. It didn't "fit" until after Jesus rose from the dead. Then and only then did the disciples understand it as a prefiguring of Jesus' ultimate return to the earth in power and great glory.

Jesus knew that the three disciples could not yet understand the transfiguration and its significance. They certainly could not properly convey its meaning to the others at this time. In this passage, we again see Jesus "managing" the news and information flow. Obviously, He had a complete and perfect understanding of timing and how best to use the facts at hand. Today's leaders need to follow His example to the fullest extent possible.

Jesus provides an ideal pattern for leaders to follow. To release information not fully understood, with its implications unclear, is to create doubt and confusion instead of confidence and orderly progress. A wise leader needs to understand how valuable, even precious, information is. It needs to be seen as a perishable resource, to be used at "its peak of freshness," but not before it is "ripe."

This concept is understood so well in financial circles that there are very strict laws governing the release of information. In the past decade, several high-profile financiers have spent time in jail for misusing information and manipulating the timing of its release for their own benefit and to the detriment of others. Corporations with major announcements to make wait for the stock markets to close before making them, allowing time for everyone to receive the information and react to it in an orderly way.

Of course, Jesus used information and the news He created in ways that would advance His cause—the most noble cause ever conceived. With Jesus as their example, wise leaders will continually work to refine their communication skills.

CHAPTER 35

THE FREEDOM TO FAIL
———— MARK 9:14–29 ————

"Whenever it seizes him, it throws him to the ground. He foams at the
mouth, gnashes his teeth and becomes rigid. I asked your disciples to
drive out the spirit, but they could not."

Mark 9:18

Good leaders recognize the importance of giving their followers a chance to fail sometimes, knowing that failure is
generally a much better teacher than success. After all, if the
disciples had worked this miracle on their own, it might have
puffed them up with pride. By allowing them to fail—and in
a very public way at that—Jesus humbled them and made
them very willing to listen to what He had to say.

Note also that this "failure" comes on the heels of the
transfiguration. It's a reminder that "mountaintop experiences" are no substitute for simple faith in God, as expressed
in believing prayer. Perhaps "the boys" felt a little cocky

after Peter, James, and John shared what they had seen and heard. If so, this humiliating failure would quickly bring them back to reality.

Sometimes leaders must give their people chances to succeed or fail on their own—and then be ready to help them no matter what happens. And sometimes we must let our people fall on their face in front of many people, which, by implication, will probably embarrass us as well.

Keep the goal in view. You want leaders who can reproduce themselves in others, which means having the confidence to take decisive action even at the risk of occasional failure.

CHAPTER 36

CALL FORTH FAITH

"If you can?" said Jesus. "Everything is possible for him who believes."

Mark 9:23

Over and over Jesus demonstrates the power of words—the right words for the right occasion. He constantly shows us that leadership is much more than titles, charts, and directives. Leadership, to accomplish its highest purposes, must be based on inspired and inspiring communication.

It is easy to say that telling someone to be an inspirational leader is like telling someone to be taller. This is the easy way out, the fatalistic view. True, some people have more innate flair than others, but we can all add to the amount we have.

We need to work on inspiration to be inspired. We need to be conscious of the need to add inspirational communication to our repertoire of leadership skills. We need to "go to school on" inspirational leaders of the past. This is what we are doing with this book. We are studying the most inspirational leader of all time—Jesus.

One of the things Jesus teaches us about inspirational communication is that for us to be effective with it, we must be there. This may seem so obvious as to sound ridiculous. However, many of today's leaders fail to show up at opportune times, when inspirational communication could be delivered.

How often do we read or hear that "A spokesperson for XYZ had the following statement to make. . . ." I find myself asking, "Where's the top guy? I want to know what he says and how he says it." Leaders often miss making the impact they could by failing to put in a personal appearance in crucial situations. Hiding behind a "spokesperson" is easy, but not productive.

I think many leaders choose not to make a personal appearance because they haven't practiced and prepared for occasions when the enterprise can best be served by their presence. Obviously, Jesus was very well prepared. In an earthly sense, He had studied the Scriptures, the basis for almost all His public remarks. He had "showed up," even as a boy, to exchange views with the leaders of His day.

It is certainly true that a leader needs to be selective about showing up personally. Jesus demonstrated this brilliantly by using John the Baptist to pave the way for Him. The key here is the phrase "pave the way." A spokesperson is most useful as one who "sets up" the leader for an important communication. If John the Baptist had had the last word instead of preparing the way for Jesus to have the last word, the plan and the communication would have been incomplete.

In the passage we are considering, Jesus used the pithy phrase "If you can?" as a means of awakening the father's dormant faith. Sometimes leaders recognize potential in others that they themselves do not see or feel. The issue isn't the father's desire for his son to be made well—that much is abundantly clear by his bringing the son to the disciples in the first place. But will he now place his faith in Jesus alone, or will the disciples' failure so utterly discourage him that he won't believe anything at all?

I find the father's reply honest—and heartening. How often do we all say, "I believe—help my unbelief." All true faith is mixture of belief and unbelief. Yet that little belief was more than enough for Jesus to perform a mighty miracle of healing.

Once again we see the world's greatest leader calling forth faith from a man who didn't know he had it in him. All it took was a little phrase—a simple question—a "word fitly spoken" by the Master.

You don't have to say a great deal. Sometimes just a few words at the right moment can work wonders.

CHAPTER 37

ONLY BY PRAYER

He replied, "This kind can come out only by prayer."

Mark 9:29

To consider the leadership lessons of Jesus and not to include the importance of prayer would be unthinkable. Prayer was a major part of His life and teaching. Not to fully appreciate this is to have an incomplete and distorted picture of how Jesus lived and how He led.

He used prayer in several ways. All should be instructive to us. First of all, He was a man of prayer. He prayed both in private and in public. He used prayer to order His day. Earlier in Mark, we find that Jesus got up very early in the morning, "while it was yet dark," to pray. It was a part of the discipline of His life. Leaders in today's hectic world can use prayer as a way to structure and focus the day. This is not in any way to say that prayer is not powerful, important, and necessary in and of itself. It is. But two key ways to use prayer are to begin a day and to bring closure to a busy day.

Secondly, Jesus was *an example* of a man of prayer. His disciples, those He led, had to have been struck by this. They saw what a major part prayer played in His life, adding to the confidence they felt in following Him.

Even in today's cynical world, we believe that followers in every area of life will have a higher level of confidence in a leader who includes prayer in his or her life. Certainly, there will be those who sneer. Lose an important account and someone will be sure to say, "Well, the old man's prayers didn't help us on that one." Fail to reach a fund-raising goal, and the equivalent of "Maybe we should have worked harder and prayed less" will probably make the rounds. All this notwithstanding, most people would rather follow a leader who is a man or woman of prayer.

Jesus also taught about prayer. The Lord's Prayer is the best example of this. To some it may seem sort of fey and otherworldly to teach about prayer in today's situations. Of course, prayer *is* otherworldly. That is one of the most important reasons to recommend it.

More and more people in every walk of life are looking for the transcendent. All the New Age hype and interest in pseudo-spiritual things is evidence of this. A leader who teaches the basics of true prayer to the true God cannot go wrong.

In the key verse, Jesus demonstrated the absolute necessity of prayer in some situations. There will be times when the most appropriate thing a leader can say is, "Without God's intervention, this won't happen." Some things can only be brought about by prayer. Jesus seemed to indicate that from time to time we will encounter a "this kind" of problem—some situation so overwhelming that it simply outstrips our resources. God brings us "this kind" of problem so that we will learn and relearn that our dependence must be on God alone.

Loneliness and isolation are major problems for people in business, particularly those who must travel and be apart from their families. Wise leaders will point their key people to prayer as a most effective way to combat this. It fell my lot to be one of the first Americans to go into the People's Republic of China after the end of the terrible "Cultural Revolution" in that country. I was going in, not as an American, but as the head of an international sports organization. (This was before there was a functioning American embassy there.) A condition of my entering the country was that I go alone; the Chinese were very wary of foreigners in those days.

The evening before I was to board a People's Republic government jet in Tokyo to fly to Beijing, Akio Morita, the legendary founder of Sony, graciously gave me one of Sony's most sophisticated shortwave radios to take in with me. He said, "Once you get in the Chinese jet, you will be completely cut off from any communication. You won't be able to reach anyone outside China. With the radio you will at least be able to hear from people outside China."

Mr. Morita was wrong. In the isolation of China, I was able to reach my heavenly Father more easily and directly than ever before. I had no phone or fax, but prayer more than sustained me during those strange days. I missed my family and friends, but prayer kept the loneliness at bay.

There is no substitute for prayer—especially when we face the impossible problems of life.

CHAPTER 38

THE INNER CIRCLE

They left that place and passed through Galilee. Jesus did not want

anyone to know where they were, because he was teaching his disciples.

Mark 9:30–31

Some leaders resent the time taken away from "real work" to teach and train those they lead. In our own company we have to battle the tendency to schedule "work" sessions even during our corporate retreats. We reason that we cannot afford to take time away from the basics of our business.

Leaders need to learn from Jesus. His example shows that teaching is not an interruption of the mission, but *it is the mission.* As leaders internalize this and make it the center-piece of their leadership style, great progress is made. Wise, effective leaders make sure that teaching has the highest possible priority.

Much conventional wisdom would say that as Jesus moved through Galilee, He should have taken the opportunities to address the crowds He could easily attract. Make the pitch, sell the product, influence the masses, make the numbers count, take it to the streets—these are often seen as imperatives by many leaders.

We see Jesus taking the exact opposite approach. He turned aside from the multitude of potential "customers" in order to teach His small band. What a powerful, potent, pointed lesson for all leaders!

Because Jesus placed a higher priority on teaching His disciples than on communicating the message to the masses, untold millions around the world and down through the ages have been blessed. The marvelous things the disciples were able to do after Jesus left them were the result of His putting teaching them first on His agenda. The church that blesses the world today, and which will continue to do so until Jesus comes again, is the result of this strategy.

Jesus was actually *reteaching* what He had already taught them previously. The disciples had a hard time grasping how suffering and death (much less a resurrection) could fit into God's plan for Jesus. Several commentators note that all three synoptic Gospels emphasize that the closer Jesus came to His final week in Jerusalem, the more time He spent teaching His disciples in private. This of course would climax in the great upper room discourse (John 13–17) on the night before He died.

The disciples seemed to be afraid to ask Him about His coming death and resurrection. Perhaps they thought the whole subject too morbid. Maybe they couldn't figure out what questions to ask, or perhaps they feared being rebuked as Jesus had earlier rebuked Peter. At this point, it's instructive that Jesus is content to simply reiterate His earlier teaching. No doubt He knew of their confusion, but didn't try to "force the issue." Patient teaching, repeated over time, would eventually help them understand. But in the end, their faith would be severely tested—and even shattered—by His death. No amount of teaching could fully prepare them for what was to come.

Jesus at this point gives them as much as they are prepared to receive. Later He will teach them much more. But for the moment He leaves some questions deliberately unanswered. This is also good leadership strategy.

Mass communication and the constantly emerging technology which makes this more and more powerful should certainly be co-opted for today's enterprises. We must use these tools as effectively as possible. However, it is more important to remember that the most effective teaching is always based on this rule: "The smaller the number, the more powerful the communication."

Jesus preached to the masses, but He *taught* His disciples. He saved His most important teaching for only three of these: Peter, James, and John. When He wanted to be sure an important point was made, He went one-on-one with them.

Leaders need to be sure that while they are utilizing all the communication tools at their disposal, they are giving the highest possible priority to teaching those few closest to them. A leader needs to plan for those times when he does "not want anyone to know where they are" so he can teach. No phones, no faxes, no E-mail, no "work" agendas—just teaching.

The results of this kind of teaching priority will be long-range and far reaching. It is the way Jesus led.

CHAPTER 39

THE SERVANT LEADER
MARK 9:33–37

"If anyone wants to be first, he must be the very last, and the servant of all."

Mark 9:35b

After all Jesus has said and done—after all His miracles and the repeated teachings—what were these guys talking about on the road? They were arguing about who was the greatest. Unbelievable!

In the Jewish society of that day—as in most societies in every generation—there was a huge emphasis on power, position, prestige, and titles. "Who's number one?" is still the operative question. Because He knew their hearts, Jesus knew about their sinful ambition even before He asked what they were arguing about. Like little children caught misbehaving, they were ashamed to answer Him.

At that point He could have rebuked them again, but instead He chose this moment for an unforgettable teaching experience. He did it by giving another of His pithy sayings: "To be first, you must be last."

None of Jesus' leadership lessons may seem more paradoxical than the servant/leader concept, which is, in fact, the very essence of both His leadership example and His leadership teaching. The concept of the servant/leader is difficult for many to grasp at the end of the twentieth century, in part because today's leadership literature espouses just the opposite and glorifies a different kind of leader altogether. Literature extolling Atilla the Hun, telling us "you don't get what you deserve, you get what you negotiate," and generally teaching a me-first, in-your-face, slash-and-burn leadership style is the norm.

To think that a leader can succeed by putting his or her followers and customers first, both individually and as a group, seems wrongheaded, unworkable, and a formula for failure. In fact and in truth, this leadership lesson of Jesus is the single surest formula for success ever enunciated. It is a guarantee of success in the broadest, most lasting sense. Think about it. If you are leading a company and you put your employees, colleagues, and customers first, you are on the road to success. On the other hand, if the bottom line comes first, no matter what, you are likely headed for abuses and disaster.

The lessons of Jesus only *seem* to be paradoxical. They are, in fact, clear-eyed, ultimately workable, and eminently practical. Best of all, they work in time and for eternity.

Putting others first and becoming the servant of all does not mean going soft and namby-pamby. Jesus certainly never taught that or demonstrated that. He did not come to satisfy every whim or to meet everyone's perceived need. He did not condone or put up with position jockeying, personal aggrandizement, selfishness, or greed. Hypocrisy, arrogance, and pride generated His disdain. He was forceful and direct when confronting attitudes and actions that were in opposition to both His overall mission and His followers' ultimate long-range good.

Too, it is obvious that He looked for and expected continual improvement in the disciples' understanding and action. He taught to accomplish this. He led to obtain this result. Jesus shows us that he who serves best and teaches best *leads* best. Discipline, administered through thoughtful rebukes, was a part of His servant leadership.

Serving all, in the way Jesus teaches, is not only about washing feet; it is also about leading followers into commitment, into dedication, into discipline, and into excellence. Strangely, it is in the church where this kind of servant leadership is most rarely seen. Many pastors and church leaders seem to expect to *be* served, with the programs of the church revolving around showcasing them. On the other hand, there are almost no expectations for the rank and file of church members beyond the hope that they will show up and contribute funds. The word *discipline,* clearly called for in the New Testament, is almost never even whispered.

No one is putting others and the mission first in the way Jesus taught. The kind of leadership He calls for is costly in the kind of commitment it takes and in the kind of discomfort it produces. It is, however, true servant leadership. It does produce success.

In the kingdom of God, the way up is down. Jesus overturned contemporary notions of power and replaced them with the paradox of servant leadership. In a sense He was saying, "It doesn't matter who has the title. Look for the one with the servant's heart, and there you've found your leader." As in all other areas, He Himself is the perfect example.

CHAPTER 40

CHILDREN ARE
WELCOME HERE
MARK 9:33–37

"Whoever welcomes one of these little children in my name welcomes me;

and whoever welcomes me does not welcome me but the one who sent me."

Mark 9:37

"We are a business, not a charity." This was the reaction of a corporate chairman, when looking at a board meeting agenda prepared by his assistant that had a line item reading "Children." The company did not sell products for children, but was primarily engaged in working with Fortune 500 companies and their marketing. The chairman could not see why he and the board should waste time talking about children. His attitude was wrongheaded and went against the leadership lessons of Jesus.

Both by His teaching and His example, Jesus underscored the importance of children. Again, it might seem paradoxical, with so much to do in so short a time period, that He would take so much time to talk about children, use children as a positive example, and spend precious time with them. A key to understanding this is to understand that children were not ancillary to His mission; they were an integral part of it. "Children" should be a line item on the agenda of every leader.

Regardless of the enterprise you are leading, your primary question should always be, "How does what we do affect children?" This should be a leadership question because it is right, because it follows Jesus' teaching and example, *and* because dealing with it will, in very practical and tangible ways, contribute to success.

Children are not primarily a charitable issue or a social issue. They are primarily a leadership or an enterprise issue. The more you consider children and their needs, the more successful your leadership will be. Too, you and those you lead will feel much better about both the enterprise and yourselves if you have dealt with the "children question."

First, consider the children of those involved in your undertaking. Ask, How will our schedules, what we ask of the people involved, impact the lives of our children? Also ask, How can we be a positive influence on children at large? These are questions for every enterprise. Leaders take note. I hope it is needless to say here that we should never, never exploit children. Both the public at large and law enforcement agencies come down particularly hard on those who use children for ill-gotten gain. Just ask those hapless executives who allowed their company to try to pass off colored water as juice for children.

Unfortunately, in many churches children and their needs are the last to be considered. Choice people to minister to them, their programs, their classrooms, and their supplies are considered last. They should be first. The so-called "seeker-friendly" churches have proven that if a priority is given to great programs for children, the adults will flock to that place. Churches whose programs are so demanding on adult members that their children are neglected do not succeed. They go against a principal leadership lesson of Jesus.

Tragically, leaders of churches and schools today must be cognizant of the threat that children can be abused while in their care. Without becoming paranoid, leaders must be very prudent in safeguarding children against deviants who might target churches and schools as places to gain access to them.

We sometimes sing "Jesus loves the little children." How do we know that? Because He took a tiny infant in His arms and used him to teach important spiritual truth.

As a leadership principle, this is one of our Lord's most powerful object lessons—one that still stirs the heart two thousand years later. In almost every church nursery there is a picture of Jesus holding a baby, surrounded by His disciples. It is an image that has helped to create hospitals, orphanages, infant welfare societies, Sunday schools, and children's missionary agencies around the world.

Jesus loved the little children, and so should we.

CHAPTER 41

THE "NOT INVENTED HERE" SYNDROME
MARK 9:38–41

"Teacher," said John, "we saw a man driving out demons in your name

and we told him to stop, because he was not one of us."

Mark 9:38

The "not invented here" reaction to good ideas is a problem with which all leaders must deal. In selling television advertising, we came to believe we had to convince most advertising agencies that what we were proposing was really their idea in the first place, if we were to have any possibility of making a deal.

Many very good ideas are lost, or end up benefiting someone else, because of the "not invented here" prejudice. Some people have an attitude which says, *If we didn't think of it, it must not be any good.* Leaders must fight this and convince followers to accept and co-opt good ideas from all sources, giving credit where credit is due. A way for a leader to engender this very productive practice is to recognize and reward people who are committed enough to discern a good idea and to champion it even though it originated with someone else.

Competition in and of itself isn't wrong or evil. But when all you do is count "nickels and noses" or when your only measure of success is the bottom line, you risk measuring everything you do by the standards of the world.

This passage reminds us that God's work is far bigger than our limited vision. God has His people in many places—often doing things that we ourselves could never do. When the disciples come complaining about this man who worked miracles but not under their jurisdiction, Jesus basically says, "Leave him alone." He doesn't say, "Make an alliance with him" or "Invite him to join us." It's simpler than that. "Just leave him alone. Let him serve Me in his own way."

By implication, the message is, "You take care of your business and I'll take care of Mine. Stay focused on the mission. If I need to say something to that man, I'll do it. Don't you worry about it. Do what I've called you to do, and don't forbid others from doing what I've called them to do."

A corollary concern for leaders is keeping individuals and groups within the organization focused on the mission. It is possible to do this and even to sharpen the focus by setting up internal competitive situations. Sales contests, quality-control contests, safety contests, customer satisfaction contests, attendance contests, etc., are all tried-and-true methods of energizing an organization. A leader's responsibility, however, is to monitor these kinds of efforts very closely, to keep the intensity at the right level, and to be sure everyone's focus is on the ultimate overall good of the organization and its mission.

Corporate annals are full of stories detailing how internal competition, both group and individual, got out of hand. The internal battles became so intense as to become unhealthy and detrimental to the overall effort. Any sort of sabotage, whether by word or deed, must be dealt with very severely. It cannot be tolerated.

Jesus demonstrated over and over a resolve to complete His mission. He was focused. This focus extended to making the best possible use of those who could help. His relationship with John the Baptist is the best example of this. A lesser leader could have seen John and his disciples as competitors. Jesus saw them as important adjuncts and continually praised John. He helped His own disciples to see that others doing good things in His name were to be encouraged, not discouraged.

Some churches have a particularly difficult time with this concept. They become so intense about their own programs, their own numbers, and their own parochial interests that they miss being a part of what God is doing all around them. Wise church leaders will not let this happen.

One of the most positive and productive things about the Promise Keepers movement is that, for the most part, churches have not seen it as a threat, but as a very positive program to be co-opted for the benefit of their men, their church, and ultimately for God's kingdom. The same attitude needs to prevail when God is using Young Life to win young people, or Bible Study Fellowship to disciple ladies, or Campus Crusade to reach college students. When leaders focus on God's kingdom and make sure that is the focus of everyone else, good things happen. The same principle applies in every organizational situation.

CHAPTER 42

HOW TO DISPENSE REWARDS
MARK 9:38–41

"I tell you the truth, anyone who gives you a cup of water in my name

because you belong to Christ will certainly not lose his reward."

Mark 9:41

Determining who is to be rewarded and to what extent is, at once, one of the great joys of leadership and one of its most demanding tasks. If you do it well, with discernment, it can be one of the most powerful and effective tools in your leadership arsenal. If you do it poorly, even with the best intentions, it can be a source of consternation, upset, and disunity. The phrase "High risk, high reward" could have been coined to describe the process of determining rewards and allocating compensation. Fortunately, Jesus is a rich source of help and insight for leaders who have rewards to distribute, and everyone does.

Perhaps the first thing to learn about all types of rewards is how important they are. No leader can afford to take them lightly. Wise leaders consider them prayerfully.

The second thing to understand is that money, while usually the most important reward a leader has to dispense, is far from the only one. Leaders who do not understand this are at a significant disadvantage as they deal with compensation issues in their organization. Obviously, monetary rewards had little, if any, part to play in the earthly leadership of Jesus. He rewarded His disciples in other ways—time with Him, unique experiences, great teaching, the privilege of ruling with Him in the kingdom, rich relationships to replace the ones they had lost, sharing with Him in His coming glory, an intimate knowledge of God, and the ultimate gift of eternal life. Some of His rewards were immediate, while many others would be given over time; and the greatest of all His rewards would come not in this earthly life but in the life to come. Jesus offered His followers many rewards which far outweighed the cost of their commitment to Him.

The life and leadership of Jesus teaches us another profound lesson about rewards that goes directly against conventional earthly wisdom. On the surface, it seems naive and counterproductive. On closer examination, it makes ultimate good sense and should form the basis for every leader's reward system.

Conventional wisdom says that to maximize profit, people should be paid as little as possible. Its proponents ask,

"How little can we give this person and still retain and motivate her or him?" Jesus teaches us to ask just the opposite question: "What is the *most* we can afford to give this person and be good stewards of resources and see the enterprise succeed as it should?" Basing our compensation system on the wisdom of Jesus is the most practical and profitable thing we can do. How much, not how little, should be the basic approach to our compensation considerations.

Jesus also teaches us that a static system of compensation will never be best. Some leaders would like to reduce all issues to a cut-and-dried formula. While it is possible to use salary schedules, percentages of profit, and other objective standards, a wise leader will know that no system, no matter how detailed or elaborate, can ever answer all the compensation questions. Again, one reason is that rewards are not all financial or quantifiable in terms of money.

Even where money is concerned, Jesus teaches us that leaders should have latitude in how it is paid. After they meet their obligation to pay what they say they will, wise leaders will be sure they retain enough latitude in how compensation is distributed to make the best use of it. Remember, rewards are not only given for past efforts, but also to motivate and energize toward future success.

Leaders must also learn that the rewards at their disposal are always finite. This means that you cannot give to one person or one group without taking away from another person

or group. This makes all compensation questions more difficult and calls for thoughtful, prayerful leadership.

Even leaders whose compensation pool is made up of
nonmonetary rewards need to understand this. Only one
scholar can be given the top prize. Attention given to one
person in a Sunday school class is attention not available to
others. A pastor's time devoted to one parishioner is time
not available to others. Leaders who understand this and do
their best within this reality succeed and do so with greater
equanimity.

Jesus teaches leaders that "fairness," in the way that the
world understands fairness, is not a totally operable concept
in distributing compensation. In a real sense, He came to do
away with "just rewards." He offers mercy instead of justice.
Even in our small human compensation responsibilities, we
need to move beyond the strict fairness template. As in His
parable of the workers paid equally, Jesus teaches us that
what might seem to be "fair" might not be right or best as far
as compensation is concerned.

To the extent we can, we need to view compensation on
an individual basis through a leadership lens which helps us
to see what is best for each person *and* for the enterprise.
This is not easy, but the best leaders move beyond a simple
formula.

Just as Jesus did, and just as He taught in His parables,
leaders should be able to articulate a rationale for the way
they distribute compensation. When the inevitable question

comes, you should be able to explain why. Your answer may not satisfy the questioner, but it needs to be honest, direct, and defensible in terms of the most good for the enterprise and for the people involved.

Those who cannot accept the rationale might move on. This is okay and should be anticipated. It is not a reason to change the best compensation system which has been thoughtfully and prayerfully considered.

It's also instructive that Jesus here clearly teaches that no good deed will go unrewarded. Even such a tiny thing as a cup of cold water will be noticed by the Lord. Such a "trivial" gesture seems small by the world's standards, but it goes to the heart of what it means to be a servant. Sometimes leaders make the mistake of only rewarding huge accomplishments, the winning of big accounts, the closing of big deals, and so on. But in such a system only the superstars will be rewarded. Wise leaders will also find ways to reward their "cup of cold water" employees.

Rewarding those we lead is a very complex leadership responsibility and privilege. Jesus is the best model to go to for guidance.

CHAPTER 43

THE MILLSTONE WARNING

"And if anyone causes one of these little ones who believe in me to sin,

it would be better for him to be thrown into the sea with a large millstone

tied around his neck."

Mark 9:42

What is a millstone? It's a huge, heavy circular stone used to grind grain into meal. Usually it was three to four feet across and one foot thick. Donkeys would be attached to the millstone and walk in a circle, slowly grinding the grain. Now imagine attaching such a stone around a person's neck and throwing him in the sea. He would sink to the bottom and suffer a horrible death by drowning. There would be no possibility of escape.

Such a fate would be better than the fate prepared for the man or woman who harms others under their care. Note that the warning is to protect the "little ones who believe in me." This is Jesus' way of protecting the most vulnerable among His followers — the poor, the untaught, the socially disadvantaged, the children, and any other powerless people.

Leaders who accept authority must realize that with authority comes responsibility. Leaders are held responsible for the actions and attitudes of those they lead. They set the moral and spiritual tone for their enterprise. These are among the great prices leaders must pay.

Even with the most godly and consistent leadership at the top, some people may still do bad things. After all, Judas betrayed Jesus after being with Him for three years. Our responsibility as leaders is to be sure that we are not the *cause* of a follower's failure. Part of creating and maintaining the right kind of atmosphere is a zero tolerance for evil within the organization. Many leaders have gotten into trouble by "looking the other way" when knowledge of wrongdoing within their organizations comes to their attention. This *causes* others to consider similar nefarious actions. Never ignore, never cover up, never excuse, and never delay rooting out bad things in your organization. Always deal with them immediately.

Leaders of churches and educational institutions have a particularly awesome responsibility. Strict adherence to Scripture should be a threshold requirement for all those who are entrusted to teach. If a pastor knows that a Sunday school teacher is causing the truth of Scripture to be doubted, or if a college president knows that professors are causing students to question their faith and nothing is done, leader responsibility goes off the charts.

The warning is severe. God will not deal lightly with leaders who abuse or neglect their followers. Better not to be a leader than to hurt those entrusted to your care. This should be a matter of daily prayer.

CHAPTER 44

TAKE UP YOUR AXE

"And if your foot causes you to sin, cut it off. It is better for you to enter

life crippled than to have two feet and be thrown into hell."

Mark 9:45

This verse is, perhaps, the strongest statement on focus in all of the Bible. Jesus is admonishing us all to keep foremost in our thinking the most important goal of every life—to live in intimate fellowship with God. *Anything* which might cause us to miss this goal must be put out of our lives.

Maintaining focus is one of the most important ongoing responsibilities of leadership. It begins with a mission statement and continues as we compare what we are doing and planning with that mission statement. We must be ruthless in discarding those activities and programs which do not contribute directly to the goal as outlined in the mission statement. This sounds easy, but it is not. It is the leader's responsibility to maintain focus.

Consider a Sunday school class which is formed with a very simple mission: to study God's Word. One hour a week is set aside for the sole purpose of Bible study by a homogeneous group. There is a simple mission with a very sharp focus.

Here is what often happens. Someone says it would be nice to open the class with a song or two. Fine. The class begins with singing.

A suggestion is made that the class should promote "fellowship" among its members. Fine. Time is set aside at the beginning of the class for coffee and fellowship. Class time is taken to discuss and plan for fellowship opportunities outside of class. ("Should we have a potluck or a picnic? How does two weeks from Friday fit into everyone's schedule? How about three weeks from Friday?")

The church leaders recognize that many who come to Sunday school do not stay for the worship service so they see class time as perfect to make general announcements. Time is set aside for this.

Since the Bible admonishes us toward good works, the class decides it should support a charitable endeavor. Which one? How much should be given? When can someone bring a report on how our money is being used?

You get the idea. The focus on Bible study, the real purpose of the class, has been lost. Bible study is, at best, relegated to a lesser role; and the goal of a discipled class has been dissipated.

Maintaining focus can be both costly and painful. It won't be easy for that Sunday school class to regain its original vision—especially when those other "worthy" goals have been added. The human tendency is always to drift away from our original commitments. But when we sense that happening, the cost of moving against the tide will be enormous. It's like cutting off a hand or plucking out an eye.

You can't do that kind of surgery without great pain. That is why some churches, colleges, and organizations drift endlessly for years and years, and in the end bear little resemblance to what they once were. No one is willing to get out the axe and start hacking away. But that is precisely what must be done.

By the same token, this passage has a great deal to say about leaders who come into organizations that have drifted and lost their vitality. You'll need many things to revive your company—faith, patience, wisdom, a winsome spirit, a long-term focus, an ability to separate the trivial from the crucial. All those things are needed. But remember what Jesus said. Take a sharp axe with you to work. Sooner or later you're going to need to start chopping away at the things you don't really need. You can't get back on track without it.

Focus is about making sure only the *best* goals are pursued. "Best" must be defined as those goals most consistent with the mission statement. Maintaining focus needs to be an ongoing, daily discipline for leaders.

CHAPTER 45

WORTH YOUR SALT

"Salt is good, but if it loses its saltiness, how can you make it salty

again? Have salt in yourselves, and be at peace with each other."

Mark 9:50

Both in this passage and in the Sermon on the Mount, Jesus used the salt metaphor very powerfully. Leaders of today, in all kinds of enterprises, need to appropriate this lesson.

In biblical times, salt represented the faithfulness of God. Salt reminded the Israelites of how faithful God had been to them, how He had kept His promises. Today's leaders need to be faithful, to be faithful to their mission, to those they have asked to follow them, and to the standards of godly leadership. Nothing harms an enterprise and those involved in it more than the unfaithfulness of a leader.

As moral absolutes have been leached out of our society, we have seen more and more leaders of business and industry fail the faithfulness test. They have been unfaithful in ways which range from outright stealing to managing the enterprise for their own personal gain rather than accomplishing the mission for the good of all involved. Some have been personally unfaithful in leading lives outside the office which have brought public shame to them, their followers, and the enterprises they have been chosen to lead. Tragically, leaders in and of the church have far too often been unfaithful in exactly the same ways as those with other leadership responsibilities.

Leaders and those who hold them accountable need to understand that they must adhere to a high standard of faithfulness. They need to be able to say to those who follow them, "I have been faithful. I expect the same from you." When a leader cannot make this statement, an essential leadership asset is gone and much of the high ground of leadership has been lost. It is almost impossible to recover.

A line from the great Steve Green song should be the motto for leaders of today: "May those who come behind us find us faithful." It should be a part of our daily prayer to God.

As Jesus spoke about salt, He also had the other metaphorical uses of salt in mind. Salt adds flavor, a tang of excitement to food. What an important lesson! Leaders need to be alert for ways to make their enterprise interesting and exciting for those involved. Leaders need to see that followers do not settle into a dull routine, a kind of "another day at the office" syndrome. When this happens, effectiveness is lost and energy levels go down.

Obviously, the excitement factor is easier to maintain in some enterprises than in others. A major league baseball player has more inherent excitement in his job than a guy making widgets in a factory in Peoria, but a part of every leader's responsibility is to generate excitement for the mission, whatever it is. My dad was in the paint manufacturing business all his life. This might seem to be the epitome of dullness. But because my dad understood the importance of his product in the lives of people, he was passionate about it and made it interesting and exciting to those involved. Every leader needs to be able to make the enterprise's purpose known and meaningful.

Certainly, those who are involved in the work of the church should never be bereft of interest and excitement. Their mission is the most exciting, challenging, and vital of all. The consequences of what is done or not done are paramount and eternal. Excitement and vitality should reign. Sadly, this is often not the case. An attitude of "same old, same old" often prevails. Church leaders cannot, must not, let this happen on their watch.

Leaders in the church need to be excited themselves and to generate excitement in those they lead. Otherwise, such banal considerations as worship style and the next budget campaign become the focal point of the church. Leaders need to focus on the life-changing, destiny-affecting role of the church and display it constantly before all involved. Otherwise, keeping the organizational machinery running becomes the uninspiring goal.

Jesus also taught about the preserving aspect of salt. While demonstrating faithfulness and generating excitement, leaders need to be sure they are working to preserve the things that matter most in their enterprises. This is an admonition of particular importance for leaders coming into a new situation. In an effort to make needed changes and generate new enthusiasm, be wise in preserving the good already there.

As a college student, I had a firsthand experience with a leader who did not understand the necessity of preserving the good things of the past. A new president came to the college full of passion for the job and determined to move the institution forward. In his zeal to do this, he mandated many changes. Some of these were changes in the decades-old traditions of the school, which were precious to students, faculty, and alumni. Enthusiasm for the new president turned to outright rebellion, and he was gone in a very short time. He failed to understand a leader's responsibility to preserve the good things of the past. Do not make this mistake as you lead.

The salt metaphor of Jesus was powerful in His day. It should be just as powerful in the lives of today's leaders. Be faithful. Be excited. Be preserving.

CHAPTER 46

MARRIAGE AND LEADERSHIP

"Therefore what God has joined together, let man not separate."

Mark 10:9

It is no exaggeration to say that we were made for marriage. When all is said and done, and when the final count is taken, most people will be married at some time. Not that marriage is better than singleness. It all depends on the two people who are married and the one person who is single. Many people can best fulfill God's will for their lives by remaining single forever (1 Cor. 7:7–8). Others may choose to marry later in life. But that should not obscure the main point: *Marriage is one of God's best gifts to the human race.* Proverbs 18:22 says, "He who finds a wife finds what is good and receives favor from the Lord." Hebrews 13:4 adds that "Marriage should be honored by all."

The statistics bear this out. Even though the divorce rate is soaring, marriage is more popular than ever before. Consider the following: There are twice as many married men as single men, almost ten times as many married men as divorced men, and twenty-three times as many married men as widowed men. Among both men and women in virtually every age category, those who are divorced and widowed remarry at a higher rate than never-married people do.

What does all this have to do with leadership? Jesus used a question by the Pharisees as an occasion to teach His followers about the sacredness of marriage and the danger of divorce. Marriage was God's idea in the beginning. The notion of one man with one woman for a lifetime goes all the way back to Adam and Eve in the Garden of Eden. God intended that they be joined together in a relationship so strong that it could only be called "one flesh."

By contrast, divorce was man's idea, a product of the hardness of human hearts. Every person who has been through the breakup of a marriage understands what Jesus means. Though there are times when divorce may be necessary because of sinful behavior, it is never painless or easy.

In our day—when divorce has become so common— leaders must do all they can to create a corporate culture in which marriage is upheld and honored. This may pose a problem because our society increasingly has moved away from a biblical viewpoint. In the secular arena, Christians will work side by side with others who may have radically different perspectives on marriage and sexual morality in general. How do you uphold the sanctity of marriage in a pluralistic setting?

The answer is not difficult. Maintain the strength of your own marriage. That means always speaking well of your spouse, making sure that people know you are married, and taking time to nurture your own relationship, even if that means taking some time away from work to be alone together. It also means recognizing the possibility of temptation in the workplace and intentionally setting some "fences" that will protect you from a foolish mistake that could ruin your career and marriage and lead you away from God.

There is a very real sense in which a Christian marriage is a "window in time" through which others catch a glimpse of eternity. We are like actors on a stage with the whole world watching. Our marriage is our starring role. When a husband plays his part well, when a wife plays her part well, the audience sees something deeper; they see Christ and the church. That's the way God set it up, which is why a Christian marriage either draws people to Christ or drives them farther away.

And that is why there is no such thing as a private divorce. If we think it makes no difference if we get a divorce, we are wrong. If we think it is nobody's business but ours, we are wrong. The whole church is involved. God's reputation is at stake.

All around us marriages fail. You hear about it every day. You may work in an office where you are the only person still married to the same man or the same woman. Sometimes you hear about another divorce and you hardly know what to say. People get divorced for the flimsiest reasons.

Here's some exciting news. You are a missionary to that office . . . and your marriage is your message. You don't have to preach a sermon. *Your lifetime commitment to your husband or wife is a visible sermon that people see every day.*

How can you show God's love to others? Let them see it in your marriage. It's more effective than a hundred tracts or two hundred Scripture verses. *People may doubt the things you say, but they cannot deny the reality of a truly Christian marriage.*

Marriage matters to God, and it ought to matter to you. When leaders keep their vows, it becomes easier for followers to keep their promises.

CHAPTER 47

OVERPROTECTING
THE LEADER

People were bringing little children to Jesus to have him touch them,

but the disciples rebuked them.

Mark 10:13

Overprotection is a problem every leader faces eventually. In fact, it's probably true that the more successful you become, the more likely it is that your key people will go out of their way to shield you from unwanted distractions. In the beginning of any dream, leaders will often be found talking with anyone about anything because they aren't encumbered with a staff to manage, a budget to maintain, and a heavy schedule to keep. In the early days leaders *have* to be accessible, if only because they have no one else to talk to and nothing else to do.

Little by little things change. You find a few key people who will join you in your endeavor, you begin to define your goals more precisely, and over time an organization begins to develop around you. You establish procedures, set office hours, and eventually write a policy manual. All of those things are good because they keep you (and your organization) focused on your mission.

However, even the best things in life can sometimes become obstacles. If your policy manual keeps you from seeing people you need to see, then it's time to change the manual.

No doubt the disciples meant well when they tried to keep people from bothering Jesus with their children. One can even imagine them saying, "Look, it's not that Jesus doesn't like children. He *loves* children. It's just that He's busy right now and can't be bothered." That sounds good, and it might have worked until Jesus Himself intervened. Verse 14 tells us that Jesus was indignant. One translation even uses the word *irate*. He interrupted His men, took the children in His arms, put His hands on them, and blessed them.

There are times when a leader must do what only a leader can do. Sometimes you have to cut through the red tape of procedure, even if it means embarrassing your top people in the process. You'll actually create a teachable moment they will never forget.

Take a lesson from Jesus. Don't let anyone "overprotect" you from the people you truly need to see.

CHAPTER 48

THE TRUTH ABOUT FLATTERY

MARK 10:17–31

"Why do you call me good?" Jesus answered.

"No one is good—except God alone."

Mark 10:18

Jesus' conversation with the rich young ruler has generated much controversy. The rich young ruler used the term *good teacher* in a rather flippant way (v. 17). Jesus' reply on one level means, "Do you have any idea who you are talking to?" The man evidently saw Jesus as a gifted, Spirit-led rabbi who had unusual insight into the ways of God. But Jesus was not satisfied with that level of understanding. "Don't call Me 'good' unless you know who I really am." Jesus refused flattering comments from people who barely knew Him.

This man was trusting in his own innate goodness to get himself to heaven. He truly thought he had obeyed God's commandments perfectly from childhood (v. 20). Thus, he not only misunderstood who Jesus was; he didn't have a clue who he himself was. He was wrong on both counts—stemming from a defective view of "goodness," which for him was a kind of relative outward morality. He was good by his own moral code but was a sinner by the standards of God's perfection.

Contrary to the assertions of hostile critics and cults, in this passage Jesus is not denying His Deity as the Son of God. Elsewhere in Scripture Jesus clearly asserts Himself as the Son of God, the Messiah. As He answers the rich young ruler, in a subtle way He is trying to lead the man to see the truth of His sonship—and at the same time refusing to accept cheap flattery.

Jesus never varied from His mission. One part of that mission involved making sure people knew who He was and why He came. To that end, Jesus corrected misinformation and always gave God credit and glory.

Leadership by its very nature generates positive comments. The better you do your job, the more praise you receive—and the greater the possibility of being badly misunderstood, and of having flattery turn your head. Some leadership positions need to be sort of glamorized for the enterprise to succeed. Leaders in these kinds of positions need to be especially alert to flattery's seductive nature. To put this admonition in the vernacular, "Don't get sucked in."

Or to use the words of Jesus, which are always better, "Woe to you when all men speak well of you. . . ." (Luke 6:26).

Be aware that flattery is a weapon of the enemy. It can lead to arrogance, and arrogance is deadly.

One of the best weapons leaders have to combat a tendency toward arrogance is to keep in mind a clear picture of Jesus kneeling to wash the feet of His disciples.

CHAPTER 49

LEADING VERSUS MANAGING

MARK 10:32–34

They were on their way up to Jerusalem, with Jesus leading the way, and the disciples were astonished, while those who followed were afraid. Again he took the Twelve aside and told them what was going to happen to him.

Mark 10:32

Note the timing here. At this point in Mark's Gospel, the die is cast and Jesus knows that He is going to Jerusalem to be crucified. The leaders of the nation have hardened their hearts against Him. Nothing can change the ultimate outcome.

Ever since Peter made his magnificent confession in Mark 8:27–30, Jesus has been dropping hints along the way. He knows what lies ahead and, like any good leader, He begins to let them in on the secret bit by bit. He has waited until now because, frankly, His men couldn't take it any earlier—and they can barely stand to hear it now.

Now that the time has come, Jesus is specific with the bad news. He identifies exactly what will happen, who will do it, and what they will do to Him—spit on Him, flog Him, and kill Him. No doubt this shocked His disciples, but it also gave them enormous confidence because they knew He wasn't caught by surprise in Jerusalem. He walked into that city with His eyes open. He predicted it, and it came true just as He said.

Picking the right time to tell what you know can generate enormous confidence in your followers and give them courage when the hard times come. Even so, the disciples were "astonished" and "afraid." Real leaders often astonish and frighten as they lead. They break new ground, take new territory, and ask for new kinds of commitments. They make new kinds of commitments themselves. Maintaining the *status quo* is what managers do. This is not at all a bad thing, but it is not leadership. Leadership, by its very definition, means being out front blazing new trails. This always causes amazement, fear, and discomfort. The leader is almost always the one who is called upon to give the most.

This passage should call potential leaders to ask themselves some very fundamental questions. The first is: "Am I willing to lead—really lead?" In business, education, and the church, I have seen what happens when people have aspired to leadership positions, attained them, and then refused to lead. When their organizations "were on their way up to Jerusalem," they were not leading the way.

When those who have leadership positions refuse to lead, all kinds of bad things ensue. Decisions aren't made and communicated. Roles aren't defined. Assignments are not made. Discipline is not maintained. Order is not kept, and direction is lost. Their organization never gets "to Jerusalem."

Please do not seek or accept a leadership role unless you are willing to put yourself on the line by making the tough calls and the toughest commitment yourself. Leaders must lead, and it is a difficult and demanding role.

The second question this passage asks potential leaders to consider is: "Am I willing to think of new ways of doing things? Can I think outside the box and color outside the lines? Is it possible for me to astonish some people and even cause fear in others?" As always, Jesus is the example. He was the most revolutionary thinker of all time. He asked His followers then, and asks us today, to think in completely new and different ways. "If it's not broke, don't fix it" is not a motto for leaders. A leader should see every enterprise as "broken" to the extent of asking the questions, "How can it be done better?" and "Are there new and untried ways we can use to improve?" This is what leadership is about. Managers accept things as they are. Leaders do not.

There is a third very important question this passage asks leaders to consider. "Am I willing to be open enough, vulnerable enough, and intimate enough with a core group of followers that I can share bad news with them in a timely way? Will they have learned enough about the mission and my commitment to it to still follow me 'up to Jerusalem' after they have heard it?" Some leaders don't engender enough confidence in their followers to feel they can handle bad news and tough times, so they only dispense good news. This is not the way Jesus led. He continually told His disciples both about the coming kingdom and about the terribly high cost of bringing it about. This is a lesson for all leaders.

As you lead and consider leading, ask yourself the questions this passage evokes.

CHAPTER 50

TOTAL COMMITMENT
MARK 10:35–45

"What do you want me to do for you?" he asked.

Mark 10:36

James and John came to Jesus seeking the ultimate no-cut contract, the quintessential golden parachute. They wanted Jesus to promise them, on the spot, based on what they had done in the past, untold future riches. What they got was a wonderful leadership lesson from Jesus. It is a lesson from which we can all profit.

No matter what kind of group you lead, you will have, or be perceived to have, largesse to distribute. You can be sure that your followers will come to you in the same way that James and John came to Jesus, seeking to make the best possible deal for themselves. By using Jesus' example, you can make the situation profitable for all concerned and, at the same time, move your mission forward.

First of all, Jesus heard them. He listened to them. He didn't say, "Your request is ridiculous. Get outta here." He asked them to go into their request in more detail. In doing so, He learned a lot. He learned something about their opinion of Him and of His power and authority. This told Him a great deal about the two men and about how much they had grasped of what He had been trying to teach them. He had to be pleased with what they had learned, if not with their selfish motive.

If an employee comes to a corporate leader and asks for guaranteed future pay increases, that is one thing. If he comes asking for a guaranteed pay increase based on the profitability of the company, that is something much more in favor of the employee. The request which puts the employee in the most favorable light is the one which asks for a future raise based on the *increased* profitability of the enterprise or the *increase* in its stock price. This signifies that the employee is not trying to renegotiate based on past performance, but is saying, "I believe in this company and am willing to work hard to make it even more profitable. I want to share in its success."

A wise leader will follow the example of Jesus when followers come seeking increases based on past performances, and he will present future challenges to them. James and John came asking for a great deal. Jesus challenged them to earn it by performing through future difficulties. This is a terrific way to handle those who come to you. It provides you with insight about their confidence in the enterprise and in you as a leader. It asks them to increase their commitment. It provides them an incentive to do better for a longer period of time.

Good leaders don't sugarcoat the commitment they seek. Jesus took the brothers' request at face value and challenged them to join Him in an incredible adventure that includes sacrifice beyond anything they have experienced so far.

When Jesus asked, "Can you drink the cup I am drinking?" He was in essence inviting them to come and die with Him. Here we come to the bottom line of life. "Are you willing to sacrifice everything that is dear to you in order to follow Me? If the answer is yes, then you can also share in the rewards."

This has huge implications for leadership. First, you've got to be involved in something worth a total commitment. Second, the leader must himself have made a total commitment. You can't ask people to do what you haven't done yourself. Third, the followers must be challenged to give all they have in the hopes that by united effort, some goal may be accomplished together that could not be accomplished individually.

These are not words to toss around lightly. You only make this kind of challenge when you have found something worth giving your life for.

—————————— CHAPTER 51 ——————————
THE ROYAL ORDER
OF SERVANTS
——————————MARK 10:41–45——————————

"Not so with you. Instead, whoever wants to become great among you

must be your servant."

Mark 10:43

Now the disciples have started to argue among themselves, which shouldn't surprise us. The whole episode begins with the strange request of James and John and ends with a heated dispute. It's all perfectly natural because we were born to compete, to fight for the top spot, to look out for number one. Winning and losing is what it's all about. Whether we admit it or not, getting ahead of our friends is a major motivation in everything we do. Before we condemn the disciples, we ought to take a good look in the mirror.

Jesus didn't condemn them. He used their bickering as an occasion to challenge them to channel their ambition in a brand-new direction.

Ambition has become something of a dirty word in our day. To many people it implies an overwhelming desire for personal advancement regardless of the cost—and regardless of who is hurt in the process. Let's face it. There *is* entirely too much of that kind of ambition in the business world. In every company or office you can almost always find a few people who are willing to play fast and loose with the truth if it will help them climb the corporate ladder. They cut corners, they lie on their expense reports, they spread malicious gossip, they abuse their authority, and they know how to stab you in the back and walk away laughing.

Jesus knew all about men and women like that. And He understood that His followers would be tempted to use the same tactics. With four simple words He radically broke with that kind of ambition: "Not so with you." Then He painted an entirely different picture of ambition. "Do you want to be a leader? That's great because the world needs good leaders. Here's what I want you to do. Become a servant. Pick up a towel and start washing dirty feet. Think of yourself as a slave and not as a master."

No doubt the disciples recoiled at the thought of taking the menial role of a servant. After all, these were the geniuses who had just been arguing about who was going to have the seat of honor at the big banquet in the kingdom. The whole point of picking the seat of honor is to have someone else serve you.

"Not so with you." With those four words Jesus turned the values of the world upside down and established a new fraternity—the Royal Order of Servants. Want to join?

True leadership is not a matter of having a title, a position, or an overwhelming personality. *Leadership is first and foremost a matter of the heart.* Who is the leader we need? The one who is a servant. Find the servant, and you've found your leader. He's not the big shot sitting at the head table. He's the one out in the kitchen serving the meal.

CHAPTER 52

TAKE TIME FOR PEOPLE

MARK 10:46–52

"What do you want me to do for you?"

Mark 10:51

For days and weeks Jesus has been on a journey toward Jerusalem. He has an appointment with destiny in that city. The storm clouds of angry judgment are gathering on the horizon. He knows what is ahead. Because He is the Son of God, He sees with perfect clarity everything that is about to happen—the plot, the thirty pieces of silver, the traitor's kiss, the late-night arrest, the trials, the false accusations, the scourging, and the crown of thorns. Most of all, He sees the cross clearly and knows that in just a matter of days He will hang there, suspended between heaven and earth.

This is why He came to earth. This is what the Bible means when it says that "his hour" had finally come.